little bits
QUILTING BEE

little bits
QUILTING BEE

20 QUILTS USING CHARM SQUARES, JELLY ROLLS, LAYER CAKES, AND FAT QUARTERS

by **KATHREEN RICKETSON,** *founder of WhipUp.net*

Illustrations by Robert Shugg
Photographs by John Paul Urizar

CHRONICLE BOOKS
SAN FRANCISCO

Color Catcher is a registered trademark of Glanmire Industries Ltd.
Jelly Roll and Layer Cake are registered trademarks of United
Notions, Inc. Popsicle is a registered trademark of Unilever Supply
Chain, Inc. Special thanks to the following companies: Susan St.
John Interiors, Le Forge, and La Maison.

Library of Congress Cataloging-in-Publication Data available.
ISBN: 978-0-8118-7730-5

Manufactured in China
Designed by Sarah Pulver
Styling by Stephanie Powell

10 9 8 7 6 5 4 3 2 1

Chronicle Books LLC
680 Second Street
San Francisco, CA 94107
www.chroniclebooks.com

4-11-16

CONTENTS

INTRODUCTION

WHAT IT'S ALL ABOUT

For me, crafting is a personal creative and artistic journey that luckily has a practical application. Whipping up a pair of pajamas for my kids on demand (I have a no-fail pattern in my head), making a new quilt for my growing son, or helping my daughter with her numerous creative experiments—all of this is in a day's work for this crafty mama. Sure, spontaneous making and crafting for the family helps me be a good mom. But I also need to tap my clever, cool, artistic inner self, and that is where making my own quilts comes into play.

Designing and sewing the quilts in this book has been a rich and fruitful journey—one that began in 2001 with my first quilt and my discovery of the handcraft blogging community. Making that first quilt was agony, filled with unrealistic expectations of perfection. After I finished, although it was a proud moment, I didn't make another quilt for quite a while. I made that first quilt the hard way, with too little skill and without the right tools for the job (where was the basting spray, why didn't I know about the freestyle embroidery foot, and why oh why didn't I have a rotary cutter?).

Now here I am, many quilts later. I've wended my way through the quilty world and found my confidence; discovered the buzz you get from making quilts. I've obsessed over (and written a book on) mini quilts and learned new skills and methods. With each method found, I've refined

my quilt-making approach, and built up a stock of preferred techniques, tools, and products. Hopefully this book will provide a shortcut for you as you embark on your own quilting journey; I wish I had had it 10 years ago.

As a busy working mother, my quilting time is limited to my days off, evenings, and the odd rainy weekend in between shouts of "Mum, how do I do this" and "Kath, where do I find the . . ." I have to divide my time (as many of you do) between motherhood, work, house, garden, and my other hobbies. In order to finish my projects in a timely manner, I've developed a quilting style that involves lots of shortcuts, which is why using pre-cut fabrics is right up my alley! When I was asked to write a book about using pre-cuts, I was excited, and realized it was the perfect opportunity to share my new quilting methods and shortcuts. The techniques, tools, and materials in this book are perfect for the crafter with limited time and space, who wants to experiment with fabrics and quilt-making but doesn't necessarily have weeks to do so; it's also perfect for the experienced quilter who has done the hard yards with tricky piecing and hand-sewn seams and wants to have some fun playing with fabric.

The projects in *Little Bits Quilting Bee* are divided into four chapters, each using one of the most popular pre-cut fabric sizes for quilt making: 5-in/12-cm Charm Squares, 2½-in/6-cm Jelly Roll Strips, 10-in/25-cm Layer Cakes, and 18-x-22-in/46-x-56-cm Fat Quarters. Each section includes patterns for five quilts and offers a variety of quilt styles and difficulty levels. If you've never quilted before, start with the easier quilts such as Aloft, a quilt for baby, or Crimson Cross, a full-size bed quilt, which use a very easy block design. These quilts will get you started on basic block sewing. As a beginner, please don't fret over wonky seams or matching corners—little imperfections not only add to the charm of a handmade quilt, but are essential to accept if you're going to enjoy the process. Seams will become neater and corners will match as your skills improve. Once you've mastered a few techniques, you can confidently tackle more difficult designs such as Step Lively and Dress Circle. These intermediate quilts will introduce you to simple appliqué and different layout designs. If you want more of a challenge, try Summer Sundae, Pop Wreath, or Garnets and Gold, all of which will get you sewing with triangles, curves, and hand-sewn appliqué. In the equipment section, you'll find ideas to help you organize your work space and make your limited time more efficient and effective.

DESIGN INSPIRATION

Inspiration hits me at random moments and in strange places. All of a sudden, I need to reach for my notebook in the supermarket line to sketch the skirt of the woman in front of me, or pull over to the side of the road while driving to jot down a sentence that popped into my head. I get in a flurry about all sorts of things—words, pictures, sounds, feelings, and textures; keeping a journal helps. I also have an inspiration wall in my craft space where I pin up my collection of vintage postcards, art exhibition invitations, my favorite hand-sewn vintage quilt blocks, or a found hand-tatted doily. Mixed into all of this inspiration are photos of my children and their incredible drawings. Surrounding myself with so much color and vibrancy transports me briefly to another place and allows me to be inspired by the genius of others.

Some of the designs in this book were triggered by small sparks: 5 Flavors is inspired by candy packaging, Summer

Sundae by the name of the fabric range Sweet, and Lollypop Tree by my dreams of growing lollypop trees! Others were inspired by Amish quilts, antique quilts in history books, even vintage postcards. When I'm open to it, ideas follow me; the quilt designs in this book are a collaboration with my kids, my collections, and my crafty pals in blogland. This is a crafty adventure I'm on, sometimes exciting and challenging, but mostly rewarding and energizing. I'm excited to share it with you in this book!

COMMUNITY QUILTING

This is a book about making quilts with shortcut methods and pre-cut fabrics, but it's also about learning together, sharing ideas, and helping each other—in fact, that's what the craft community is all about.

TRADITIONAL QUILTING BEES

The romanticized version of the quilting bee brings up lovely visions of quilting tea parties and ladies in the drawing room gossiping around the quilting frame, but this is only one version. Sometimes a bee is just a few women getting together at the local church hall on a regular basis, or a gathering of the top stitchers in the neighborhood working together to complete a special occasion quilt. The quilting bee, throughout history, has been an opportunity for women to get out of the home to exchange recipes, news, gossip about children, learn new skills and swap patterns and fabric, all while finishing quilts. In short, it's a forum for women to help and support each other.

It's funny, the traditional quilting bee sounds a bit like online craft communities to me; both are about teaching, learning, and sharing knowledge. Of course, women (and occasionally men) do still get together to quilt—there are hundreds of quilting guilds in America alone. But the online quilting community has the added bonus of being global and having access to an incredibly diverse pool of ideas, traditions, and histories. Online, you can get involved in quilt-alongs, quilt block and fabric swatch-swaps, and charity quilt drives; join virtual quilting bees; and meet like-minded quilty folk.

VIRTUAL QUILTING BEES

Virtual quilting bees are like traditional quilting bee parties in principle—they consist of an online group (between 12 and 16 members), where each member contributes toward a quilt for each of the other members. When it is your month, the rest of the group makes a block or two in a prespecified color range, fabric range, or block design, then mails the finished block(s) to be combined together into one quilt. If it all works out, each member of the group gets a turn to have the other members make blocks for her quilt. There are many variables with a virtual quilting bee (just as there are with a quilt), and it is up to the group to work out the specifics beforehand. Skill levels are not generally an issue, but if you're joining a group that's been quilting for a while, you might need to prove that you're up to the job and that you're committed to the group before you're accepted.

Starting your own virtual quilting group takes organization and commitment. Having a strong online presence helps, only because others may already be familiar with your work. As the Twelve by 12 group did (see facing page), you could reach out to a small select group of artists whose work you admire, or you could put out a general call for participants. It might be a good idea to select a theme. Themes are very helpful, and can add a cohesive element for groups working together for the first time. Tight themes can help beginners to focus their efforts. For experienced quilters, a loose theme offers plenty of leeway for fun interpretation.

To get started, try Flickr.com, a hub for these groups, as well as various forums and online quilting groups. See Resources.

SWAPS

The Charm quilt, made up of many pieces of fabric in a single shape (a square, hexagon, or triangle), became popular just over 100 years ago when printed fabrics first became widely available. Charm quilts were often composed of hundreds or even thousands of pieces of fabric without repeating any. To complete one of these quilts, it was essential to swap and share fabric scraps, often through the mail. This process was facilitated by popular quilting magazines at the time and swapping Charm Squares became a big fad at the end of the 19th century.

The online craft community has embraced the swapping and trading tradition and taken it to new heights. Now there are even Web sites specifically set up to facilitate swaps, such as www.swap-bot.com/ where you can swap pieced patchwork blocks, vintage fabrics, scrap packs, Charm Squares, and even mini quilts. These swaps not only help you acquire a wide variety of fabric scraps to add to your stash, but are also a great way to get involved with the online quilting community.

HOW DO SWAPS WORK?

To join a swap, sign up at the organizers blog, craft forum thread, or Flickr group, and follow the rules set by the organizer. You may be allocated a partner or several people, or asked to send your items to a central person who then will arrange the items and send them out to everyone (you might be asked to contribute postage costs).

QUILT-ALONGS

For quilt-alongs, a group selects a quilt pattern from a magazine or Web site and the members make the quilt simultaneously. The group gets together throughout the process at each other's homes to assist each other in understanding the pattern instructions and learning new techniques.

An online quilt-along is usually started by a blogger who has a design she wants to share. She posts a challenge to her readers to make the design along with her and each week discusses another step in the process. Hundreds of people make the quilt at once and there are often dedicated group blogs or Flickr groups set up so everyone can share their progress.

Joining a quilt-along is easy—there are no fees or memberships; you just have to check in each week to read the weekly lessons. These quilt-along challenges are an incredible resource for new quilters. Some quilt-alongs will have detailed instructions on making binding or how to stipple quilt, while other quilt-alongs will assume that participants have that knowledge, and just give the basics to make the patchwork blocks and put them together into a quilt top. There are many quilt-alongs where a group of quilters sets out to make all or some of the quilts from a popular quilt book, and others that act as a support group where members encourage each other to complete unfinished quilts or to use only fabric scraps.

GUILDS AND SEWING CIRCLES

Quilting guilds have a reputation for being traditional and strict about doing things the "proper" way, but in reality they're incredibly social, provide classes, have guest speakers, run quilt shows, and organize charity quilt drives. In 2009, the Modern Quilt Guild was started to counteract the problem of younger women finding a suitable quilt guild; it now has chapters all over the world. With this guild, modern quilters, whose previous outlet was only the Internet, can connect with like-minded folks in their area, who are not fussy about straight seams, traditional designs, or mitered corners. See Resources for more information.

FROM THE COMMUNITY

Katie Starzman shares a blog with her creative twin sister Laura; together they explore their creativity and make and sell their creations online. They share their ideas with each other and the blogging community through their blog Duo Fiber Works.

I belong to a weekly knitting group. When one of their members shared she was pregnant with her first baby, the group, inspired by the concept of community quilts and the stories of women building community as they quilt together, organized a crib quilt project. My sister, also a member of the group and a textile artist, hand dyed the fabric and was the main project manager, while the rest of the group, all beginner quilters, were the quilting worker-bees. Our knitting club turned into a weekly quilting bee party. Working on the quilt together was a lovely experience, something I've wanted to do for years. It's such a connection to pioneer women who saved scraps to make blankets to warm their families, to my mom and her friends who had regular quilting bees, and to the new babies who will be swaddled in the cozy blankets. I love everything about it!

KATIE STARZMAN
www.duofiberworks.com

BLOCK CLUBS

BLOCK-OF-THE-MONTH CLUBS

These clubs, often published in quilt magazines and online newsletters, include a monthly mail-out of fabrics, a block pattern, and instructions. Many of these quilts are sampler quilts that involve hand stitching and appliqué and are meant to be long-term projects. Most block-of-the-month clubs require a joining fee.

SATURDAY SAMPLER CLUBS

Saturday sampler clubs are similar to block-of-the-month clubs, except that a quilting shop usually runs them. The idea is that members go to the shop weekly for a set period to pick up the next week's quilting homework. These clubs are enjoyable because of the social aspect. Plus, the quilt shops often include a day course to kick things off and finish with a show-and-tell party.

I encourage you to join a quilt-along, sign up to a quilt mailing list, or buy into a block-of-the-month club—you will be motivated, improve your quilting skills, and meet some great new people in the process.

FROM THE COMMUNITY

Aurora Ann Fox is a quilter from Alaska who has been involved in community quilting for many years. She shared this amazing experience with me:

In 1985 during the Cold War before communist Russia fell, I organized a Peace & Friendship quilt. I sent out blank quilt squares to all the quilters and artists I knew in Alaska, and to some Quaker groups. Women in my community approached me and offered to help me sew the quilt top and quilt it, so it became a real community project. I had each person who created a quilt block write a note about why they made their square.

Once it was finished, I traveled to Siberia to present it to the Russians as a peace gesture. At first I had no idea how I would get the quilt to Russia. About 2 months into the project I found out that an Alaskan friend was organizing a group of performers to travel to the Soviet Union and perform. When I asked her to take the quilt she said, "Why don't you come along and bring the quilt yourself?" This trip changed my life. We gave the quilt away in Siberia in Irkurtsk from the "people of the tundra (Alaska) to the people of the tiaga (Siberia)." I learned from The Peace Quilt Project that each small action we take does make a difference.

One of the biggest rewards for me was two 13-year-old girls in my community telling me "we are so glad you are making this quilt, because we don't want any wars." If all I did was give them that hope and plant that seed for peace, I knew what I was doing made a difference.

AURORA FOX
www.foxyartstudio.blogspot.com

FRIENDSHIP QUILTS

Friendship quilts, also known as signature quilts, autograph quilts, or album quilts, have been around since the mid-1800s. They were made to record relationships, friendships, and memories or for charity and community commemorative pieces. These types of quilts use a simple construction and are generally made with signed quilt blocks. Each block is lovingly made by hand by a different person, often with inscriptions or Bible quotes embroidered into pictorial appliquéd histories. These are now considered valuable historic documents.

My fascination with friendship quilts led me to organize a friendship quilt project for this book. I wrote to some of my blogging cohorts and sent them a little pack of fabric and a block pattern and asked them to embellish however they liked and then sign it. The resulting Across the Globe Friendship Quilt includes more than 20 participants. I really enjoyed the process—it was the perfect way to commemorate this quilting journey. You and your friends should try this, too!

ACROSS THE GLOBE FRIENDSHIP QUILT

This quilt pattern is suitable for making with a group of friends or extended family. It would also make a great school or charity project. I used a pack of pre-cut Jelly Roll strips—this helps to hold the quilt together with a common color theme—but feel free to use scrappy strips or ask your friends to provide their own strips (thus personalizing the quilt even more). I also used unbleached muslin cut into 10-in/25-cm squares. Off-white or white fabric is good for adding embellishments, but you could also use a pack of pre-cut Layer Cakes squares.

MATERIALS

1 pack of pre-cut Jelly Roll strips (2½ in/6 cm wide)

20 (or as many people as you have participating) squares of 10-in/25-cm off-white cotton fabric

EMBELLISHMENTS

Buttons • yo-yo's • ribbon • lace to personalize your square • embroidery floss or perle cotton and/or fabric pen that won't wash out (to sign your name)

MAKING THE QUILT

1. Make up the block as per the basic block directions in the Crimson Cross quilt on page 107. Make your block so the cross is off-center, leaving a small blank square in the lower right corner for signing and a larger blank square in the upper left corner for embellishing.

2. Trim your block to an 11-in/28-cm square. Embellish as you like in the upper left (large square) corner and then sign in the lower right small corner. Make sure you leave enough space around your design to allow for the ¼-in/6-mm seam allowance used to join the blocks.

3. The embellishing part is the fun, exciting part. Some of the friends who made blocks for this quilt pieced the large top section; others used stamps, appliqué, and embroidery. The variety and creativity that came out of this project were astounding.

4. To complete your friendship quilt, continue by following the quilt directions on page 107 for the Crimson Cross quilt, which uses this simple block design. How many squares you have will depend on how many people participated—you might end up with a lap quilt or a king-size bed quilt.

NOTES

- Use ¼-in/6-mm seam allowances throughout.
- Pieced block measures 11 in/28 cm square; finished block size is 10½ in/26.5 cm square.

FROM THE COMMUNITY

Mara Otterstad is a keen crafter who has participated in a family quilt challenge each year for the past 10 years.

We have an annual multi-generational family quilt challenge that happens every year. The family meets at my grandmother's retirement village in Arizona to reunite from around the country and decide on next year's challenge. It is amazing to see how we each interpret the challenge and just how different everyone's quilts turn out. This annual event keeps the family bond strong as we are all scattered across the United States.

Each year is a new challenge for our skills and abilities. We each try something new as presented by the challenge and learn from each other's strengths. The "show and tell" is also a neat way to get feedback on our quilting skills. It is very encouraging to get positive comments and suggestions from people who also quilt, especially in a safe setting with family. The sense of belonging is very significant in choosing to participate in the quilt challenge. It is something to talk about, commiserate about, and celebrate with the friends and family who participate. My great aunt mentioned to me that she invited her daughters-in-law to participate to give them a new way to bond with each other. I thought that was really special. Here we are, four generations sharing in a common activity to bring our family together.

MARA OTTERSTAD

CHARITY OR FUNDRAISING QUILTS

Women have been making quilts for charity as long as they have been making quilts. The Civil War in America brought out the best in quilters all over the country. Massive country fairs were organized to sell thousands of quilts to raise funds for the troops.

Even before this, Ladies Benevolent Societies organized quilts to send to orphanages, communities of fugitive slaves, and missionary workers around the world. These societies would take a booth at the country fair and display a "10 cent" signature quilt. Participants would pay 10 cents to write their name onto the quilt and the quilts would be auctioned.

You don't have to be in a guild to make quilts for charity. You could send a quilt to one of the many quilt fundraiser groups (such as Project Linus) or start your own quilt drive for a local cause you believe in.

To get involved in charity/fundraising quilts, check www.projectlinus.org for a quilt chapter near you, or join your local quilt guild and get involved in the charity arm; ask your local church—many churches constantly raise money for local hospitals, shelters, and orphanages; start your own quilt for charity—post a call on your blog, Flickr group, or quilt forum.

FROM THE COMMUNITY

In 2009, U.S. quilter Tia Curtis headed up a charity quilt drive for Australians who had lost their homes in one of the biggest bushfires in Australian recent history.

My husband is in the US Army. We were stationed in Alice Springs, Australia for about 3 years. It is pretty remote out there and I kept in contact with my friends and family through the Internet. I am fairly active on Flickr and participate in the doll quilt swaps and have a couple little quilting bees I quilt with on Flickr. It made me feel all the closer to my crafty friends in the rest of the world during that time.

In February 2009, we were getting ready to move back to the USA when the Victorian Bushfires happened and charred much of Victoria, Australia. It was heartbreaking to hear about. Homes were not just burning, but exploding. 200-year-old Gum trees were turned to ash. It was devastating.

I am an Army Nurse and when I saw all that suffering I had to do something. I did not think the Victorians needed my nursing skills, but my comfort. I thought about what would be simple to do, and make a difference. Quilts! I have been quilting for years and I make quilts for the children of soldiers killed in Iraq and Afghanistan out of their fathers' uniforms. I know that these quilts bring comfort . . . they keep the connection with something tangible.

After I got the idea, I posted a little notice on Flickr: "We should make quilts for the people in Victoria." From there, the project quickly took on a life of its own. I asked for people to send me 1 or 2 liberated or wonky star blocks so I could piece them into lap sized quilts, quilt them and then send them down to Victoria so they could be given out to the people who had lost so very much in the fires.

Blogs all over the world put the word out and before I knew it, I was over my head with lovely liberated stars to make into quilts. Ladies and gentlemen from all over the planet opened their hearts and sent me blocks, fabric, thread, completed quilt tops, completed quilts. It was stunning. I initially thought I would get enough for about 3 quilts. In the end we had 128 quilts that were finished and the majority of those were trucked down to Victoria to distribute to those in need.

I did not do all the quilting myself. I joined together with the Alice Springs Quilting Guild and we had two quiltathons where we stacked and quilted the quilts. Ladies all over town had little quilt packs they were working on. This was such a great event for Alice Springs; we all came together and worked hard. It's incredible that nearly every continent contributed to this project.

TIA CURTIS
www.campfollowerbags.blogspot.com

65 ROSES CHARITY QUILT

My mother-in-law Dace and extended family are involved in the Cystic Fibrosis (CF) association of Australia. My husband has a very close-knit family; when his cousin's first baby was found to have CF, the family rallied around to not only offer emotional support but to find out more about this disease and help with fundraising and research to find a cure. When I started researching charity quilts, I decided to offer the CF foundation a quilt for their annual charity. They loved the idea, and so did Dace, who immediately rallied her friends to make blocks; at the same time, I asked for block donations on Whipup.net, and together we cobbled together this truly community-based quilt. Two of Dace's friends made the central panel using their own design. The names of all the contributors are listed on page 158 and are sewn onto the label on the back of the quilt. I sewed up all the blocks and quilted it so it was ready for auction. The result was an amazing feeling of achievement and community.

You can make this quilt for a charity of your choice. It involves a simple base block of four 5-in/12-cm squares sewn together and a rose (or design of your choice) appliquéd or embroidered in the upper left square. Once you have collected or made sixty of these blocks, arrange them around a central five-rose appliqué panel.

MATERIALS

For the whole quilt, you'll need 60 plain Charm Squares and 180 patterned Charm Squares, plus an 18-in-/46-cm-square piece of plain fabric to act as the background for your central panel.

If you're making this quilt with a group of friends, you might like to use pre-cut Charm Squares and hand them out. If, as I did, you ask the contributors to supply their own materials, for each block, they'll need 1 plain and 3 patterned 5-in/12-cm Charm Squares, plus extra fabric and thread for the rose design.

NOTES

- Use ¼-in/6-mm seam allowances throughout.
- Pieced block measures 9½ in/24 cm square; finished block size is 9 in/23 cm square.

MAKING THE QUILT TOP

1. Make up your basic block as per the diagram below, using 1 plain and 3 patterned squares; sew the 4 squares together to make a 9½-in/24-cm block.

2. Embellish with a rose design (use one of the designs offered here, or create your own) on the plain square, using appliqué, machine or hand embroidery, or cross-stitch; attach a crocheted rose; or even use fabric paint.

3. After collecting 60 rose blocks, make the central panel containing the remaining 5 roses, using appliqué or embroidery—65 roses total. In the quilt I organized, the central panel was made with 3D appliqué velvet roses, layered and attached with a pearl button in the center. Be creative—improvise the 5-rose central panel.

4. Assemble the quilt using the layout diagram, turning the blocks so that 4 roses are adjacent. Sew together and press carefully.

5. Baste, quilt, and bind the edges using your preferred methods and the instructions on pages 37 to 45.

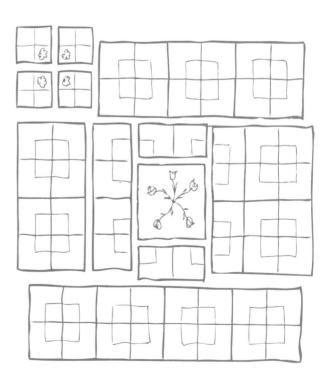

PRE-CUTS

Fabric manufacturers, and sometimes quilt shops, cut bolts of fabric from the same fabric range or color range into pre-determined sizes, then sell them in packs for quilting.

All of the quilt patterns in this book make use of pre-cut fabrics:

Charm Squares (5-in/12-cm squares)

Jelly Roll Strips (2½-in/6-cm strips)

Layer Cakes (10-in/25-cm squares)

Fat Quarters (18-×-22-in/46-×-56-cm pieces)

They all have one thing in common—they are perfect for quilt making!

PRE-CUT MYTH BUSTERS

1. *If I use pre-cuts, there's no room for individual creativity.* I think boundaries, whether self-imposed or from outside sources, can actually enhance creative thinking. With so many different pre-cuts and the number of different fabrics available, there's much room for experimentation.

2. *Prewashing pre-cuts is tedious.* Using a set of coordinated colors, such as those provided in the pre-cut packs, lessens the chance of colors running. However, if you're mixing pre-cuts with other fabrics, you should do a test swatch. If you are using solid colors or batiks or hand-dyed packs, or if your colors are dark purple, blue, or red, and you plan on mixing them with light colors, then please do prewash. Think of the process of washing these small bits of fabric as an opportunity to examine each lovely piece individually. While you're washing and ironing, you can dream and plan what you'll do with them—and think of all the time you saved by not having to cut all those squares or strips yourself.

3. *Pre-cuts are only for beginner quilters.* Advanced quilters can get as much value out of using pre-cuts as beginner quilters. Fabrics available in pre-cut bundles makes it easier to choose, and enables you to have on hand all the fabrics you need for a project. If you are an advanced quilter, you'll have more patterns and techniques at your disposal, to get enormous use out of these packs.

4. *Pre-cuts prevent you from being spontaneous with your designs.* Incredible as it may seem, you don't have to use up the whole pre-cut pack in one quilt! Why not separate them into color values and if you need purples and whites, just grab them out. Or try using half a printed Jelly Roll pack with half a solid color Jelly Roll pack. There's no rule stating that you cannot mix the pre-cut packs. Besides, many people dislike the idea of matchy color-coordinated quilts. Having a variety in your stash is certainly worthwhile and you can stock up on basics—like those Kona Solids or Moda basics in white and black—that will coordinate with other fabrics from your stash.

CHOOSING COLOR

Using pre-cuts takes away a lot of the pressure of worrying about color—however, this doesn't mean you should forget about it altogether. You might like to use a pre-cut pack with some coordinating yardage, or make your own pre-cut pack with fabrics from your scrap bin. In either of these cases, you need to be aware of color theory. Consult the color wheel and think about opposite and complementary colors. More importantly, think about for whom the quilt is being made (and why), and make sure to consider the washability and easy care of the materials when making quilts for utilitarian or more decorative purposes.

DESIGN CHECKLIST

• *Where will this quilt be used?* Is it intended to coordinate with your decor, or to add a splash of color to a plain space? Do you want soothing or energizing colors?

• *Who will use the quilt?* Your grandmother, who likes reproduction French antiques, will have different color preferences than your preteen, who only ever wears black and yellow. This might seem obvious, but often when we are making something we think about what we like, rather than what the recipient likes!

• *What will the quilt be used for?* A utilitarian everyday quilt for your son who is going away to college will require a dark background that won't show the dirt, whereas a wedding quilt is prettiest with a white or cream background.

In addition to using a color wheel, I suggest that you keep a few basic pre-cuts in your stash for this sort of decision-making. Here are some of my favorites:

Moda Jelly Roll Basics in white, milk, natural, and black. These Jelly Rolls contain 40 strips, each 2½ in/6 cm wide, all the same color—perfect for sashing in between blocks or for mixing up with your scraps.

Robert Kaufman's Kona Solids Roll Ups come in a tonal pack of 40 strips, each 2½ in/6 cm wide—each strip a different solid color. I suggest keeping sets of the brights, classics, and pastels.

Charm Squares packs of 5-in/12-cm squares in solid colors: The pastels, brights, and classic palettes work well with many different projects. I also suggest keeping packs of prints in your favorite palette, such as an assortment of plaids, stripes, and polka dots. These can be used for a single project, but are also fun for mixing it up.

PREPARATION AND STORAGE OF PRE-CUTS

Washing pre-cuts is mostly not necessary (see Pre-cut Myth Busters, page 19), but if using darks with white, then please do a test swatch. If you must prewash your pre-cuts (because you are worried about chemicals and dye runs), do so carefully to avoid fraying and tangles. Hand-wash and rinse and then either run through the dryer a few at a time, or air-dry. If you machine-wash these itty bitty pieces of fabric, the edges will fray and they will tangle up horribly, particularly the strips.

Once you have washed, dried, and ironed your bits of fabric, you can roll them up and wrap them with ribbon (although you will never achieve that straight-from-the-factory perfection), or fold them into zip-lock bags and label them, ready to use on a sewing whim.

If you decide not to prewash and are worried about the colors running in your quilt the first time you wash it, I recommend using a great little commercial product called Color Catchers or Dye Catchers. These absorb and trap loose dyes in the wash so they can't deposit their color onto other fabrics.

See Caring for Your Quilt, page 50, for more information.

EQUIPMENT, TOOLS, NOTIONS, SUPPLIES

SEWING MACHINE

Invest in a good sewing machine. It doesn't need to be fancy, but it should be sturdy (one that doesn't vibrate all over the table when you have your pedal to the metal). A secondhand machine can be excellent, but be sure to test it before buying, and get it serviced before you start using it. Another good idea is to borrow a sewing machine from a friend, so you can learn about what you want or don't want in a machine before investing in one.

All sewing machines will do the basic stitches. You might want to look for extras, such as blanket stitch and button-holes. Also, make sure that you can lower the feed dogs (see facing page); this is essential if you're doing any type of freestyle sewing such as embroidery or quilting.

It's important to care for your machine. Take it in for a regular service just like you do your car, and learn how to clean it properly. Use the small tool kit (usually a small screwdriver, lint brush, sewing machine oil, and tweezers) and manual that come with your machine to maintain it, and change the needle before each new project. Keep your sewing machine manual handy. Doing these small tasks will ensure that your machine remains in tip-top shape and runs like a dream.

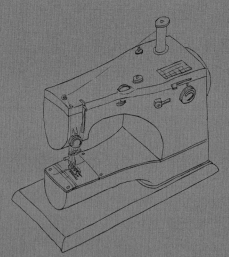

PRESSER FEET

A presser foot helps to guide the fabric under the needle and over the throat plate. There are many different feet available for different purposes; your machine should come with a few basic feet, such as a zipper foot, button-hole foot, and multipurpose foot.

A few extra feet that are handy for the projects in this book include the following:

• A walking foot is useful for sewing several layers of fabric; it "walks" the fabric so that the bottom layer of fabric moves at the same speed as the top. Use this foot when quilting straight lines or sewing binding.

• An embroidery or darning foot is used for free-motion sewing such as stipple quilting or embroidery. Use this foot when lowering the feed dogs on your machine.

• A ¼-in/6-mm presser foot is useful when accurate seams are important.

FEED DOGS

The feed dogs on your sewing machine are those metal teeth that come up through the throat plate and pull the fabric along in small incremental movements, controlling the speed of the fabric and the length of the stitches. When you lower these, you have the freedom to move the fabric in any direction. Quite a few projects in this book require you to be able to lower the feed dogs on your machine. Consult your manual for instructions on how to lower the feed dogs. Newer machines have a simple lever or setting, but if yours is an old but sturdy machine, you may need to get out the tiny screwdriver in your tool kit and remove the feed dogs manually.

BEFORE YOU START: QUICK SEWING MACHINE CHECKLIST

NEEDLES

Make sure you have spare sewing machine needles on hand. It's terribly frustrating to have your last needle break while you're in the middle of a project. Ensure that the needles you do have are suitable for the job—you should keep a supply of universal needles and some for specialized sewing, such as sharps for knit fabrics and heavy-duty needles for thick and industrial-weight fabrics.

TENSION CHECK

The upper and lower tensions must be balanced to produce a perfect stitch. If you're unsure about how to measure the tension, check your user manual. Generally, if the loops of the bobbin thread show on the top side of the seam, you need to lessen the tension; if the loops of the spool thread show on the underside of the seam, you need to increase the tension.

BOBBINS

If you are working on a large project, it's a good idea to fill a few bobbins with the correct thread so you don't have to stop and start (especially when you're machine quilting).

LIGHTING AND COMFORT

Most machines come with a small light above the presser foot, but you'll need additional lighting for working. Consider adding a good desk lamp or track lights to your work area. Make sure your work surface and chair are at a comfortable height in order to prevent bad posture and avoid a strained back.

SCISSORS

You will need three basic types of scissors: small, sharp scissors—perfect for clipping seams and precision cutting; a good pair of fabric scissors that you'll use for fabric only (buy the best ones you can afford and have them sharpened regularly); and another pair of utility scissors, which can be used for paper and miscellaneous cutting.

SEAM RIPPER

Used for undoing stitches, this small tool with a pointed tip and a small curved blade helps prevent the fabric from ripping.

ON-THE-GO SEWING KIT

A small sew-on-the-go kit is a must. Set up a jar to store your scissors, seam ripper, pins, and threads. Recycle the jar lid by gluing some wadding to it and covering with fabric for a nifty pincushion.

SETTING UP YOUR SEWING SPACE

DESIGN WALL

A design wall lets you arrange fabrics and quilt blocks on a neutral background so you can see how they work together before you start sewing. You can make a design wall with a neutral-color fabric, to which other fabrics will cling, such as felt or cotton batting.

STORAGE IDEAS FOR YOUR SEWING SUPPLIES

Stationery and storage containers are good for storing sewing gadgets, and paper envelopes are a great place to store patterns or templates. I like to use resealable plastic bags to sort everything from zippers to threads, and jam jars for leftover buttons, ribbons, and other odd bits and pieces. I also use vintage cookie and tea tins to store my cottons— I love how they look!

HANDMADE SEWING GADGETS

Try making a few helpful tools and accessories for your sewing room. Not only are they useful additions to your space, they are fun to make and use.

PINCUSHIONS

There are a lot of online patterns to help you make a groovy pincushion. Use some of your precious fabric—you will only need a little. Here are some ideas:

A Strawberry pincushion: Fill it with emery to keep your needles sharp; make it from felt and embroider little seeds all over it.

A Wrist pincushion: This is very useful when you are sewing on the go. Fill a square of fabric with stuffing, sew a button in the middle to add some definition, and attach an elastic band onto the back.

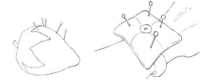

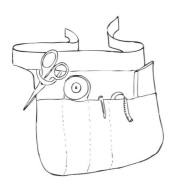

SEWING APRON

A sewing apron acts as a tool kit that you can wrap around your waist, keeping your scissors, tape measure, notebook, and seam ripper handy. Make a mini apron and personalize it with pockets and loops for your sewing needs.

THREAD CATCHER AND CADDY

These are essential to put by your sewing machine to keep your floor tidy, and drop in bits of snipped-off thread and scraps of fabrics. Make a lined bag and attach a weighted pincushion to it to let it hang from your bench. Use rice or wheat to weight your pincushion and add a loop on one side of the bag to stash your seam ripper and thread-snipping scissors in for easy access.

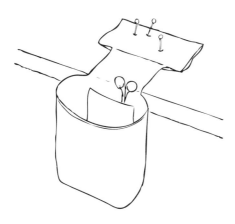

ESSENTIAL TOOLS

STRAIGT PINS

Long, sharp steel pins with round glass heads work well for quilting projects. Dull pins can damage fabrics, so keep your pins sharp by occasionally using an emery pincushion, available at sewing and craft supply stores, or make your own (see facing page).

HAND-SEWING NEEDLES IN A VARIETY OF SIZES AND TYPES

Using the correct needle for the job saves time, saves your fabric, and keeps you from swearing rather a lot while you work. Keep sharps for all-purpose sewing, embroidery needles that have a larger eye to take decorative threads, and quilting needles.

IRON

An iron is the key to creating professional-looking projects; it enables you to make neat seams. Remember to press, not glide, to prevent any stretching of fabric. An ironing board is useful, but if you don't have one, you can lay out a towel or thick fabric on a heatproof table or workbench for pressing.

ROTARY CUTTER

A rotary cutter creates a smooth, even line when you're cutting fabric. The blades are extremely sharp, so use caution. Use it with a cutting mat and thick acrylic ruler.

SELF-HEALING MAT

A cutting mat protects your work surface when you are using a craft knife or rotary cutter and has ruled lines to help guide you. Be sure to store your mat flat and don't leave it in the sun because it can warp.

MEASURING TOOLS

You'll need a flexible tape measure and at least one rectangular quilting ruler. I love my 6-in-/15-cm-wide ruler, as it's wide enough to be held firmly in place while cutting. A quilting ruler is transparent, has a wide surface, and has imperial and metric measurements. This type of ruler is essential for accurate cutting, ensuring nice straight lines when you are cutting fabric with your rotary cutter, or squaring up edges. The standard length is 24 in/61 cm, which enables you to cut Fat Quarters and 44-in-/112-cm-wide fabric, folded in half, without moving the ruler. If you are looking to expand your ruler collection, I suggest a 5-in/12-cm and a 10-in/25-cm square ruler—both are useful for cutting fabric squares and trimming blocks. A 2½-in-/6-cm-wide ruler works well for making binding strips.

THREAD

There are many types of thread available for sewing, and getting to know the best type for your projects can take a bit of experimentation. Here is a checklist to help you:

Machine sewing: It is essential to use a good-quality thread in your sewing machine for the smooth operation of your machine. You will get less thread breakage and less lint, as well as maintain good tension in your projects. Choose a thread without loose fibers. Cotton or cotton blend can be good choices for machine sewing.

Machine quilting: When you are quilting by machine, your machine is going at a fast speed and you need a strong thread that will withstand the quilting process. Choose a cotton thread specifically marked for machine quilting and purchase larger cones if you can afford to—these will save you money and time in the long run.

Hand quilting: I have recently discovered the joys of coated cotton thread especially made for hand quilting. This thread has a stiffness and solidity to it that doesn't tangle and pulls through the quilt layers easily. If you don't have access to coated thread, choose a good-quality cotton thread and run it through beeswax to prevent tangles.

Embroidery: Threads for hand embroidery come in many different guises: wool, silk, cotton, polyester, and different weights and strands. The purpose of your project will guide your choice. As you will be putting a lot of effort into your hand embroidery, choose the best thread you can afford and ensure it is colorfast.

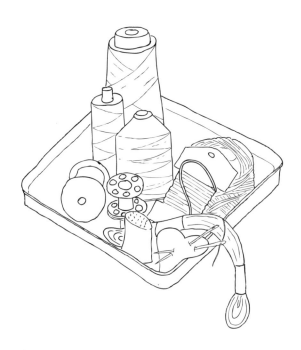

SHORTCUT TOOLS AND PRODUCTS

Each of the projects in this book comes with a list of items that are needed or that are just useful for completing that project. Many of these items are recommended for multiple projects and are useful additions to your sewing tool kit.

EMBROIDERY OR HAND-QUILTING HOOP

An embroidery hoop is basically a pair of concentric rings made of wood or plastic that holds your fabric at an even tension while you sew. You place the fabric between the rings and tighten with a screw.

BEESWAX

Beeswax is a lovely little extra to have to rub over the thread and needle when hand quilting. It strengthens the thread and helps reduce tangling.

THIMBLE

A thimble is used to protect your middle finger while you are hand sewing. Thimbles come in a variety of sizes and varieties. Try them on and select the one you find most comfortable.

BIAS TAPE MAKER

Feed your strips of fabric through this little metal gadget and, as the folded tape comes out the other side, press with a hot iron to make single-fold binding tape. These come in different widths and speed up the task of making binding.

SAFETY PINS

You'll use safety pins at regular intervals for basting, when machine quilting.

QUILTING GLOVES

Specialized quilting gloves help you to grip the fabric while you move it around, when you are doing free-motion quilting. Regular rubber gloves for gardening work just as well.

MARKING PENCILS

Fabric marking pens/pencils with water-soluble ink allow the marks to be removed later with a damp sponge; disappearing-ink pens have air-dissolvable ink; tailor's chalk will simply rub off. Whatever type of fabric marker you use, test it first on a scrap of fabric, to make sure it can be removed later.

IRON-ON TRANSFER PENCIL

These pencils allow you to trace your design in reverse onto paper and then flip the paper over and iron the design onto your fabric.

MASKING TAPE

Masking tape is useful for marking edges and straight lines.

PAPERS

Freezer paper: is a medium-weight white paper with a plastic coating on one side, used for wrapping food. When ironed, it clings to fabric, and, when removed, it leaves no residue. You'll find it in crafting applications for appliqué, templates, and stencils. You might use it as a guide for needle turning under the seam allowance for appliqué, for creating even circles for appliqué, for English paper piecing, as a backing to stabilize fabric so you can run it through your printer, as a tear-away stabilizer for embroidery, and as a stencil for fabric painting.

Paper to trace templates: Tracing paper, brown paper, and craft papers are useful to have in your craft box and for foundation piecing.

QUILT BASTING SPRAY

Some of the designs in this book recommend this as a quick and easy basting method. All products are different, so read the instructions carefully.

FABRIC GLUE

This glue temporarily holds fabric together while you sew. Choose a water-soluble glue—inexpensive glue sticks are perfect for holding pieces in place temporarily while you sew. You can also purchase special appliqué glue from your sewing shop. This glue has a handy, narrow applicator tip that allows you to dab tiny dots of glue on the seam line of appliqué pieces and eliminates the need for pins and basting stitches. I find that spray glues, including basting spray, are also very useful. All of these water-soluble glues should dissolve in the wash; check the manufacturers' instructions to ensure they will wash out easily.

FUSIBLE WEBBING OR PAPER-BACKED ADHESIVE

This is a material that fuses fabric pieces together when pressed with a warm iron. It is generally used to position appliqué pieces on quilt tops.

ANATOMY OF A QUILT

Traditionally, *there are three elements that make up a* quilt—the quilt top, which is the decorative pieced, appliquéd, or embroidered element; the batting, a soft inner layer that gives the quilt its loft, warmth, and thickness; and the backing, which is the practical element, and can be decorative or plain. The three elements are placed on top of each other in a "quilt sandwich," with the quilt top and backing facing outward and the batting in the center. This sandwich is then basted together by machine or hand, and quilted.

The quilting holds the three layers together and can be hand sewn or machine stitched, depending on your desired outcome. The binding finishes the edges neatly, and is attached after the quilting is completed.

QUILT TOP

The quilt top is the showpiece of your quilt, where most of your handwork and design elements will appear. It's usually either patchworked, appliquéd, or a combination of these and other techniques as well. You might like to use embroidery, fabric painting, or any other fabric manipulation you like—there is no end to the creative possibilities.

QUILT BLOCKS AND PIECING

Many patchwork blocks are made up of basic grid designs, with squares, triangles, and bars in a huge variety of combinations. If you want to know more about traditional block designs, access a block design encyclopedia. Quite a few quilts in this book make use of traditional quilt block designs, from a basic Nine-Patch to the standard and not so standard Log Cabin blocks and the trickier Winding Ways. The instructions for making the blocks in this book are included with the project instructions, as are the individual block sizes (including ¼-in seam allowances) and the finished block sizes (size after a block is joined to the other blocks in the quilt top). For example, a pieced block measuring 10½ in/ 26.5 cm will have a finished size of 10 in/25 cm. The block size (including seam allowance) is included to assist you in squaring up your blocks before sewing them into the quilt.

QUICK PIECING METHODS

IMPROVISATIONAL PIECING

Also known as liberated or free-style piecing or even crazy piecing, improvisational piecing involves free-form cutting and sewing of blocks or whole quilts. This free-form method of piecing patchwork enables you to follow your instinct. There are no precise blocks to cut or templates to trace; it involves spontaneous and intuitive cutting and piecing, and is a playful approach to working with fabric. Improvised blocks work well in a structured setting, or you can improvise the whole quilt. Relaxed piecing methods are used in the Crimson Cross and Squadron quilts.

FOUNDATION PIECING

This is a traditional method used to create perfect blocks every time. To make a foundation block, sew pieces of fabric onto a drawn or printed piece of paper (or sometimes muslin). This method makes working with bias-cut shapes and angular pieces much easier, as the paper foundation stabilizes the block during construction. This method allows you to construct complicated patterns easily and accurately and use up scraps. Two quilts in this book use foundation piecing—Rhombus and 5 Flavors—to create diagonal striped blocks.

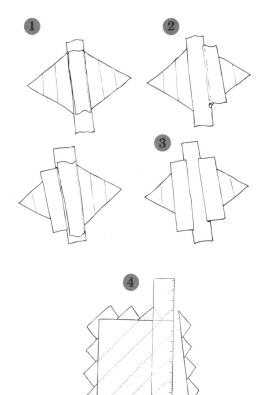

1. Place your first piece of fabric, **Wrong** side down, onto your foundation paper where marked, ensuring it has at least a ¼-in/6-mm seam allowance. It may help to secure this first piece of fabric in place with a dab of appliqué glue.

2. Place your next piece of fabric, **Right** side down, onto the **Right** side of fabric piece #1. Taking care not to move the fabric, sew on the marked line through your two pieces of fabric onto the paper foundation (see step 1 of the Checklist on page 32).

3. Press the fabric pieces open into position with a hot iron. It's important to use an iron, rather than finger pressing, to give you the accuracy that you need. Continue in this way with the remaining pieces.

4. When all of your pieces of fabric have been attached to the foundation paper, give the block a final press, and trim the edges of the block to the edge of the paper. Remove the foundation paper from the back.

FOUNDATION PIECING CHECKLIST

1. Use craft paper or blank newsprint paper as a temporary foundation. Use cotton muslin if you are planning on a permanent foundation. It's important to choose paper that will handle a hot iron and that will tear away easily.

2. When sewing your pieces to the paper foundation, use shorter than usual stitches to help perforate the paper and keep the seams intact when the paper is removed.

3. Because sewing through paper dulls your needle, you will need to use a new needle on your next project—keep this needle handy for your next paper-sewing project.

4. If you are making a lot of blocks using this method, you might like to try production-line sewing to speed up your process. This means sewing the first piece on each block, then stopping and pressing each block before continuing with sewing the next piece on all your blocks at the same time, and repeating until you have completed all the steps for all the blocks.

CHAIN PIECING

This is an efficient way to speed things up when you're sewing multiples of the same shape and size pieces. Before you start, arrange your pieces in pairs, with **Right** sides facing each other, so they're ready to go. Since you are not reinforcing the seam at the beginning and end of each block by backstitching, you'll need to use a slightly smaller stitch length than usual, so the seams don't unravel after being cut apart.

1. Feed fabric pairs through the sewing machine, one after another.

2. Sew the seams without backstitching and without stopping to snip threads; the result will be a chain of pairs of sewn patches.

3. Remove the chain of patches from the sewing machine and cut apart between each pair.

4. Press each pair flat, open or to one side depending upon your quilt design, and then get ready to attach your next piece onto these sets. You can continue in this way until you've finished the blocks.

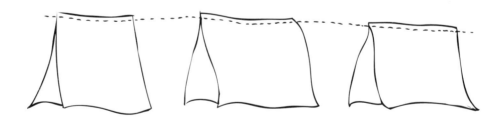

PIECING TRIANGLES

Right-angle triangles: These triangles are one of the simplest and most versatile pieced blocks you can make. By arranging your half-print and half-plain right-angle triangle blocks, you can make a stunningly huge range of quilt designs. This method is used in the Prismatic and Square Dance quilts.

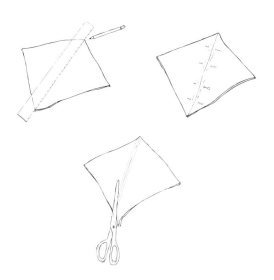

1. Place a solid-color square of fabric on top of a print square of the same size.

2. Line them up perfectly and, using a pencil and ruler, draw a diagonal line from one corner to the other.

3. Pin together, then sew a ¼-in/6-mm seam on either side of the drawn line.

4. Using a rotary cutter, ruler, and mat, cut along the drawn line, giving you 2 pieced triangle blocks, each ½ in/1.3 cm smaller than the original squares of fabric.

5. Press the seams to one side and make lots more of these.

Equilateral triangles: Equilateral triangles are also a very common type of one-block quilt. This method of sewing triangles together is used in Constructivist, Sunny Day Mat, and Summer Sundae quilts.

1. Pin each triangle to the next one along one edge; the point of one triangle should be facing up, the other point facing down—the triangles will be facing in opposite directions so that you end up with a straight horizontal line filled with triangle shapes.

2. The key to keeping points on your triangles is accurate cutting, careful pinning and consistent seam allowances while sewing.

3. It may be helpful to mark the seam allowance on the first few that are sewn, and place a pin at the point where the seam allowances come together.

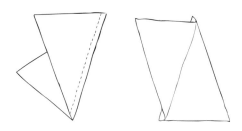

CURVED PIECING

A few of the quilts in this book make use of curves. Piecing curves can seem quite daunting, but if you follow a few basic steps, you will find it is really not that difficult after all.

1. When tracing your pattern pieces, draw registration marks through your seam lines 1 to 2 in/2.5 to 5 cm apart (closer together on tighter curves); then transfer these marks onto your fabric using tailor's chalk.

2. Pin the pieces with **Right** sides together, making sure to match up your registration marks on the convex and concave curves.

3. Sew along the seam line, removing the pins as you come to them. Then when you press the seams, they will fall naturally to the concave side.

5. Clip the seam allowance along the curves so that the curves lie flat.

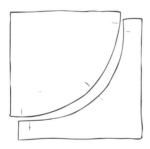

BATTING

There are many different types of batting, both fiber and thickness, and all have different purposes and advantages. Use one that is appropriate for your project, taking into consideration what purpose the quilt will serve and how you plan to quilt it. If in doubt, ask for advice at your local quilting store.

I've used cotton batting in most of the quilts in this book; it is my personal preference when machine quilting and I love the crinkly vintage appearance it gives after washing. If you will be doing a lot of hand quilting, I suggest wool batting, as the lanolin in the wool eases the hand-sewing needle going in and out of the layers. A high-loft batting will give you a puffy looking quilt, emphasizing decorative stitching, and a thin-loft will give a more antique appearance. Some drape differently, others lie quite flat, some shrink, others never do, some are better for hand quilting while others are more suitable to machine quilting. While it's a personal preference, it may take some experimentation to find the one that suits you.

TYPES OF QUILT BATTING

Bonded batting and needle-punched batting: These refer to the way the fibers in the batting are held together. With bonded batting, the fibers are held together with a glue-like bonding agent—if you don't want to use chemical additives in your quilt, avoid these. With needle-punched batting, the fibers are mechanically needle felted together. These tend to be harder to hand quilt due to their density.

Cotton batting: This is the most popular type of batting; it is soft, comfortable, and machine washable and can take dense machine quilting. It will have some initial shrinkage—hence that vintage crinkled look—and will soften with use. It is not ideal for hand quilting as it is difficult to push a needle through the dense mat of cotton fibers. Organic cotton batting is available.

Bamboo batting: Relatively new on the market, bamboo batting is eco-friendly and has similar qualities to cotton batting.

Cotton/polyester: This batting material is higher in loft than 100% cotton, but more breathable than 100% polyester. It doesn't shrink as much as cotton and is very easy to use.

Polyester: Higher in loft than cotton, polyester makes for a light, puffy quilt. It tends to be inexpensive and comes in a range of thicknesses. It doesn't shrink when machine-washed and is hypo-allergenic without the breathability of natural fibers. Polyester has a tendency to "beard" (work its way out through the weave of the fabric) and is difficult to machine quilt.

Wool: Light and warm, wool batting is very resilient. It tends to be more expensive than other fibers, but it is a hand-quilter's dream. Naturally flame-resistant, it can cause allergic reactions in some people. It needs careful washing and cannot go in a tumble dryer.

Alpaca batting: Similar to wool, but not as allergenic, alpaca batting is very expensive but oh-so-light.

TIPS FOR QUILT BATTING

• If you are using a long-arm quilting machine, or outsourcing your quilt to be professionally quilted, the batting should be 6 in/15 cm larger all around than the quilt top.

• If you are doing the quilting yourself, you should still cut the batting 5 in /12 cm larger all around than the quilt top; this gives some leeway for squaring up your quilt sandwich when your quilting is complete.

• Did you know that you can sew together your batting off-cuts to make a large usable piece? Do this by butting together two sections and overstitching with a wide zigzag, or hand sewing with a tacking stitch or ladder stitch to hold them together.

BACKING

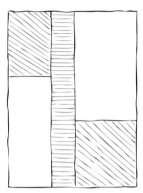

Choosing fabric for your quilt backings can be more difficult than you expect. The back of the quilt might be utilitarian, but it does look prettier if it complements the quilt front, and a pretty backing gives you two quilts for the effort of one. It's a pity to put a lot of work into the quilt top, and then use an inferior fabric on the back. It's best to use the same type of fabric (fiber content) as the one you use on the front, in order to make washing and caring for the whole quilt simpler. In other words, if you're using cottons on the front, use cotton on the back and for the binding. If you don't want to use up your designer fabric yardage on the quilt back, using a good-quality cotton sheet is a possibility; however, you'll most likely want something in between these two choices.

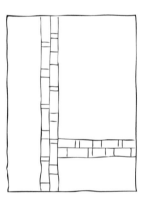

The quilts in this book all have different sorts of backing. Some are backed with pre-loved vintage fabrics; for others, I have used designer fabric yardage to make a lovely two-sided quilt. You can find extra-wide widths of fabric specifically designed for quilt backs and this can be an easy choice with no sewing required. You could make a scrappy backing, using up a whole heap of leftover fabrics, or as has been done on several of the quilts in this book, make an improvisational pieced backing using vintage fabrics, solid fabrics, and leftover scraps.

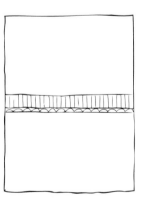

To make an improvised pieced backing using a combination of large and scrap pieces, try using the "rule of thirds"—a compositional guide used in the visual arts. Imagine the backing as an image divided into thirds horizontally and vertically; where the thirds intersect is where the interesting visual elements should be placed—creating a tension and energy. See the three diagrams at right for some ideas on how to improvisationally piece your backing. The second illustration gives just one example of how you can use the rule of thirds as a guide.

TIPS FOR QUILT BACKING

- Use a good-quality fabric of a similar weight and feel to the fabrics used in the quilt top.

- Choose a backing that has a similar depth of color to the quilt top. This makes matching the thread in the bobbin to the spool easier, preventing "freckles" of high-contrast thread from showing through when quilting.

- If you are using a long-arm quilting machine, or outsourcing your quilt to be professionally quilted, the backing should be 6 in/15 cm wider than the quilt top on all sides.

- If you are doing the quilting yourself, you should still cut the backing 2 to 3 in/5 to 7.5 cm wider than the quilt top on all sides; this gives some leeway for squaring up your quilt sandwich when your quilting is complete.

- Press seam allowances on your backing open instead of to the side to allow the quilt back to lie flat.

- If you are quilting for the first time, consider using a busy print for the backing fabric, as this will hide less-than-perfect quilting stitches.

- To piece your backing, cut off the selvages first. And sew your pieces using the rule of thirds guide, adding in scraps of fabric and contrasting colors where the thirds intersect.

BASTING

Before quilting, you will need to baste together your quilt sandwich. Basting temporarily holds the three layers of the quilt together while you are quilting. It is an important step to take, whether you are machine or hand stitching.

There are several ways of basting. Basting is usually done using long running stitches, known as "tacking stitches," over the whole quilt; however, you can also baste with safety pins placed at regular intervals. Generally, if you are hand quilting, you will use tacking stitches; if you are machine quilting, you will baste with pins. But you might like to try basting spray or a heat-activated batting instead.

1. First ensure that your backing cloth and batting are 2 to 3 in/5 to 7.5 cm bigger than the quilt top on all sides.

2. Place your backing cloth on a clean, large surface **Right** side down, smoothing it out with your hands or using a wide quilting ruler to ensure that it is wrinkle free.

3. Tape the edges of the backing to the tabletop with masking tape, to make sure it doesn't move—the tension should be even all across the backing.

4. Lay the batting on top (it should be the same size as your backing) and smooth it down. Then place your quilt top, **Right** side facing up, over the batting and smooth it out.

5. Since the batting and backing are wider and longer than the quilt top, center the quilt top evenly over the backing and batting.

SAFETY PIN BASTING

If you are basting with safety pins, place the safety pins in rows starting in the center and working your way out to each edge, pinning approximately every 6 in/15 cm.

STITCH BASTING

1. Pin the quilt, placing pins every 6 in/15 cm over the quilt.

2. Starting in the center, using a bright contrasting thread and 1-in-/2.5-cm-long running stitches (tacking stitches), follow the lines of pins, working your way out to the edge.

3. Remove the pins.

SPRAY BASTING

With spray basting, there is no need for pins and tacking stitches. This method is quick and effective and can be used for both hand and machine quilting. First, you will need to purchase a high-quality fabric spray adhesive that will wash out; ask at your local craft store for a recommendation if you are not sure which one to choose. Be sure to spray lightly; if you spray too heavily, it can gum up your needles. Protect your surfaces in case you spray beyond the edges of your quilt, and be sure to spray in a well-ventilated room.

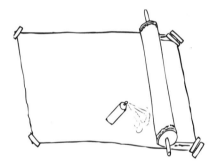

1. Lay your backing fabric, face down, on a tabletop or floor that is protected by a plastic sheet, and tape it with masking tape so it's taut all around.

2. Place your batting over the backing, making sure the edges match. While it's still in place, roll your batting carefully onto a wide length of dowel (or use a broomstick with the broom removed), and roll the batting to one end without lifting it, so that when you roll it back down, it will still be correctly aligned.

3. Spray the adhesive along the edge of the backing closest to where you have rolled the batting, and roll the end of the batting (still rolled on the dowel and still in the correct alignment) onto it.

4. Spray the next few inches of the backing, unroll the batting, and smooth. Continue to spray, unroll, and smooth your batting out incrementally until you have the whole piece of batting laid down over the backing.

5. Smooth it out all over.

6. Repeat the same steps with your quilt top; place it over your batting, centering it correctly and smoothing it carefully all over, then roll it up onto your dowel.

7. It might be helpful to tape down the far end of the fabric; this will help you roll it up without taking it out of alignment. Spray, unroll, and smooth, as you did earlier, in small increments.

8. Lift the 'basted' quilt and turn it over, smoothing down the backing one last time. You are now ready to quilt.

QUILTING BY HAND AND MACHINE

Quilting is the process of making small stitches through all the layers, to hold the quilt together and make it a sturdy, practical, and beautiful household item.

HAND QUILTING

Although it takes considerably longer, hand quilting has a special quality that cannot be duplicated by machine. I recommend hand quilting if you have hand pieced your quilt top, or if you want that extra something that only hand quilting can give. Combining machine quilting with some hand-quilted elements, or adding decorative stitches and embroidery, is also very effective. If you're not used to hand sewing, your hands will ache at first. With the help of a quilting hoop, you can take your quilting with you to the couch or on holiday, and it can be a very relaxing pastime. If you're making a very large quilt, you might want to organize a quilting bee, a wonderful way to communicate and connect, which generations of women have embraced.

To hand quilt you'll need a spot with good light, a comfortable chair, a quilting hoop, and a thimble to ensure your hand-quilting experience is enjoyable. You'll also need a quilting needle (these are called "betweens" and are smaller and stronger than normal needles). Experiment to see which length of needle feels right to you, and always use high-quality cotton thread in a coordinating color. Have several needles threaded and ready to go, so that you won't have to stop and start once you get going. You will also need small clipping scissors and a seam ripper just in case.

1. Place the area that is to be quilted inside a quilting hoop (which is the same as an embroidery hoop), smoothing it on both sides. How taut you make the fabric is a personal choice; experiment with what feels right to you, and then tighten the screw on the hoop to hold it in place.

2. Start quilting by using a hidden quilter's knot, or a few backstitches hidden in a seam.

3. Use a running stitch, pushing the needle down through all layers of the fabric (using your thimble-covered finger) until you feel it on your underneath finger.

4. Rock the needle sideways and push it up to where you want it to come back through, and continue this step until you have a few stitches on the needle before pulling the thread through.

How big you make the stitches is up to you; it's not the stitch size that matters, it's the consistency. Your hand-quilted stitches should be even and consistent on both sides of your quilt.

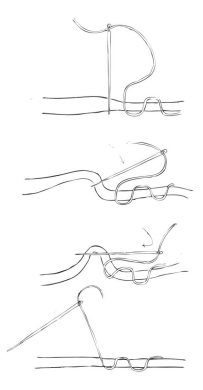

MACHINE QUILTING

Machine quilting is quick and utilitarian, but not as easy as you might think. It takes skill and patience to get the stitches even and prevent the fabric from puckering.

With machine quilting, you can also create various designs, just as you can with hand quilting, but you will need to use different presser feet depending on what you are doing.

With grids or lines, try using a walking foot on your machine. The walking foot "walks" the top layer of fabric while the bottom layer moves along with the feed dogs. You can attach a quilting guide bar to your machine to ensure that the grid lines are evenly spaced.

Free-motion, or freestyle quilting, means quilting in a rambling design all over the quilt top without stopping. Your design can be a specific pattern or one you make up as you go along. If you want to free-motion quilt on your machine, you will need to be able to lower the feed dogs. Using an embroidery foot or darning foot is also advisable. These are specifically made to be used with the feed dogs down, and they skim lightly across the fabric surface, preventing skipped stitches. With the feed dogs down, the speed with which you move the fabric controls the stitch length. Moving it at an even pace results in nice, even stitches, but this takes a lot of practice to master, so don't panic if your stitches are not uniform at first. Wearing rubber gloves or special quilting finger grips, although hot and uncomfortable, stops the fabric from slipping and helps you keep the path where you are sewing smooth.

Free-motion quilting is a whimsical alternative to structured quilting patterns. There are lots of designs to choose from. The designs used in this book are illustrated here so you can repeat them. Try an all-over random stipple, squiggle, or leaf design. The great thing about free-motion quilting is that you don't have to turn the fabric around; you just move in any direction you need. Before stitching, try drawing the design onto paper first; draw in a continuous line without lifting your pencil, and practice getting an even density.

The quilts in this book were all (with one exception) machine quilted by me. I used a variety of filler quilting designs, which are all perfect for free-motion quilting.

Scribble, rounded, and long stipple designs are perfect for an all-over fill and can be sewn bigger or closer together depending on your skill and patience and desired result. These stitches are perfect for beginners.

The two more *geometric style stitches* are also very easy to achieve and can be adapted to be sewn closer together or farther apart. I found doing the echo design to be very similar to a stipple in its execution, while the squared-off maze-like design is similar to a scribble and is fun and easy to achieve.

Cloud and wood-grain style stitches are super fun and allow a lot of freedom for experimentation.

Pebble stitch is the most time consuming of all of these. It requires a lot of going over the same area. However while it might take longer, it is very easy and forgiving—mistakes are not noticed.

The two *leaf designs* require you to go back and forth and make quick turns. They're slightly trickier and require more time to achieve as they wind around in a vine-like fashion; make big bold leaves or finer, more detailed leaves, depending on your inclination.

CHECKLIST FOR QUILTING BY MACHINE

- Wear quilting gloves.

- Oil and clean your machine before starting and be sure the bobbin tray is free of lint.

- Start with a fresh needle and have a few spares in case of breakage.

- Do a tension check on a scrap of material the same thickness as your quilt before starting, then use this scrap to practice your quilting design.

- Have several filled bobbins at the ready, so you don't have to stop.

- When you stop, make sure the needle is down in the fabric, to ensure that there are no breaks in your design.

- Begin stitching in the center of the quilt and smooth out the area you will quilt first to prevent puckering.

- Use an embroidery foot if free-style quilting or a walking foot if quilting in a straight line.

- Lower your feed dogs when free-style quilting.

BINDING

When it's time to bind your quilt, you're nearly finished! A mitered binding gives a very neat finish to your quilt. Contrasting fabric can be used to create a frame, and coordinating fabric that blends into the quilt top can be used for a more subtle finish. You might like to incorporate prairie points or bunting (see page 45) into your binding or finish your quilt with a curved edge (see page 45).

I recommend making your own binding; it's incredibly easy to do and gives you unlimited design potential; you can make it any width, using any fabric you choose, and you can make as much of it as you need. All you need are scissors or a rotary cutter, ruler, and a mat to cut the fabric into lengths. You will also need an iron to crease it down the center. A binding gadget can be handy if making single-fold binding.

WHAT IS THE DIFFERENCE BETWEEN SINGLE-FOLD AND DOUBLE-FOLD BINDING?

Working out which is which can be confusing, especially when commercial packs are incorrectly labeled. When you think of it this way, it does make sense: **Double-fold binding** has a *double thickness over the edge of the quilt.* To make, it is folded once down the center of the strip and then when sewn over the raw edge of the quilt the double thickness of fabric gives added protection. **Single-fold binding** has only *a single thickness of fabric over the edge of the quilt.* When you make it, each raw edge is folded toward the center of the strip, leaving one thickness of fabric to wrap around the quilt edges. It is used for one-step binding, for facing your quilt, or for appliqué purposes. I have used mainly double-fold binding in the projects throughout this book.

Nothing could be easier than making double-fold binding: Simply press your joined strip of fabric, with **Right** sides facing out, down the entire center length and you are good to go.

To make single-fold binding: Take your joined strip of fabric and, if you have a bias tape maker, feed one end into the gadget opening; as it comes out, the edges will be folded in toward the center. Make sure you have fed it in the right way, so that the **Right** side of the fabric is on the outside. Press it with a hot iron as you pull it out of the bias tape maker. Do the whole strip of fabric, and press it down the center lengthwise to finish. If you don't have a binding gadget, you can still make this type of binding with your iron. First press the entire length of binding down the center lengthwise. Then fold in each raw edge to this center crease and press again along the entire length.

WHAT IS THE DIFFERENCE BETWEEN BIAS BINDING AND STRAIGHT-CUT BINDING?

Bias binding is made from fabric cut on the bias (diagonal to the straight grain of the fabric). This gives the binding quite a bit more stretch, allowing it to be easily maneuvered around curves. Straight-cut binding is made from the straight or cross grain of a fabric—there is no give in this and it is used for binding straight edges.

CONTINUOUS BIAS BINDING

To make bias binding in one continuous line—without sewing multiple seams:

1. Cut a square of fabric; the size will depend on how much binding you are making (½ yd/46 cm is enough fabric for a single-bed-quilt binding).

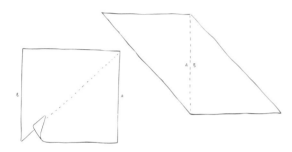

2. Cut the square in half on the diagonal, making two triangles, and sew the triangles' outer straight edges together. Press the seam open.

3. Use your ruler and a pencil to mark straight lines onto the **Wrong** side of the fabric, parallel to the long cut edges, as per the width called for in the quilt instructions. For example: For ¼-in/6-mm finished binding, you will need 1½-in-/4-cm-wide strips. For ½-in/12-mm finished binding, you will need 2½-in-/6-cm-wide strips. If you are using a bias tape maker, check what width of fabric it takes, as they come in different sizes.

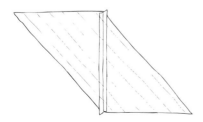

4. Sew the opposite edges of the now-sewn triangles, **Right** sides together, forming a cylinder shape. Offset one corner to match up with your line markings, and check that all the subsequent line markings also match up. Press the seam open.

5. With your scissors, start cutting at the offset corner, and continue cutting along the line markings in one continuous line until you reach the end. You should end up with a long strip of fabric that is ready to turn into bias binding. This might sound complicated, but once you have given this a go, you will never turn back; use the illustrations to guide you.

CONTINUOUS STRAIGHT-CUT BINDING

Mark straight lines on your fabric from selvage to selvage as per the width called for in the quilt instructions. Sew the selvage edges together, **Right** sides facing, leaving an offset of one line width and match up all the subsequent lines when you sew. Press the seam open. Then start to cut at the offset corner and continue cutting along the line until you reach the end. You will have a long strip of continuous straight-cut fabric ready to make into binding.

BINDING FROM PRE-CUT STRIPS

Pre-cut Jelly Roll strips (2½ in/6 cm wide) are the perfect size from which to make binding. You will need to join these strips together, end to end, with a 45-degree-angle seam. To make a strip long enough to fit around the perimeter of your quilt, measure your quilt, then add 15 in/38 cm extra to allow for corners and joining the ends.

1. Take two fabric strips and place them at right angles to each other, with **Right** sides together and the ends overlapping slightly. Pin.

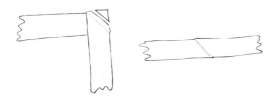

2. With your tailor's chalk, mark a 45-degree angle where the strips intersect. Sew on the marked line. Trim, leaving about a ¼-in/6-mm seam allowance and press the seam open.

3. Join as many strips as you need, then continue to make your binding using the instructions above.

ATTACHING BINDING

When you have quilted your three layers together, trimmed and squared up your quilt, and made your binding, you are ready to attach the binding to your quilt. If you are planning on finishing your binding by hand stitching, first machine sew your binding to the front of the quilt and then hand sew it down on the back, using a blind stitch or ladder stitch (see Basic Hand Stitches on page 48). If you're planning on finishing your binding by machine, with either a straight or zigzag stitch, first machine sew it down to the back of your quilt, then top stitch by machine on the quilt top.

Attaching Double-Fold Binding

1. Using double-fold binding, place the raw edges of the binding against the raw edges of the quilt top, lining up the raw edges of the quilt with one raw edge of the binding. Sew along the fold line.

2. Start sewing about 5 in/12 cm in from the start of the binding and once you go all the way around the quilt, stop just before you get to where you started sewing the binding. Trim the binding ends so that you have a ¼-in/6-mm seam allowance. Open it up and join it together, at a 45-degree angle, then place the raw edge back onto the quilt edge and finish sewing.

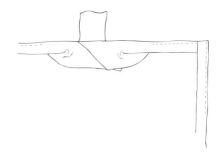

Mitered Corners On Your Binding

1. To achieve neat mitered corners when using single- or double-fold binding: As you sew up to a corner, stop and fold the next section of binding up and away from you, perpendicular to the seam; then fold it neatly back down, aligned with the next side of the quilt edge to be sewn. You will end up with a loose triangle of excess fabric at the corner. Ignore this and don't sew it down, because you will use this excess fabric when folding the corner over onto the back.

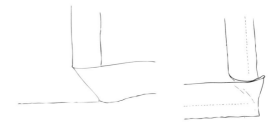

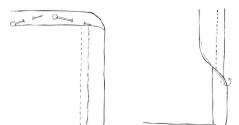

2. If you will be hand stitching your binding, turn the binding over to the back of the quilt, enclosing the raw edge, and hand sew with a blind stitch or ladder stitch (see Basic Hand Stitches on page 48). If you are planning on machine sewing your binding to finish, you will be topstitching on the quilt top; use a zigzag or straight stitch depending on the desired finished result.

PRAIRIE POINTS

Prairie points are small squares of fabric folded into triangles and sewn onto the edging, slightly overlapping each other. They make for a very pretty decorative edging.

1. Cut fabric squares; a 5-in/12-cm square makes a 2½-in-/6-cm high folded triangle. Experiment with different sizes with squares of paper first.

2. Fold the squares in half diagonally both ways and press.

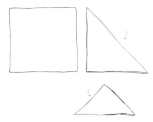

BUNTING AND SCALLOP EDGING

Bunting or scallops sewn into the edge of your quilt or into the borders makes for a very pretty and attractive alternative to prairie points. Buntings are soft and floppy and somehow romantic and modern at the same time.

Pop Wreath has lovely big scallop buntings in the binding, while Summer Sundae has irregular shaped "popsicle" buntings sewn into the border.

Make scallops by sewing two scallop shapes **Right** sides together, leaving the straight edge unsewn. Turn them **Right** side out and press flat. Place the raw edge of the buntings against the raw edge of the quilt and tack into position. Then bind, using the faced binding method.

CURVED EDGES

Curved edges on quilts make for a charming alternative to regular straight edges. Square Dance has lovely big waves and Cloud Song and Summer Sundae both have sweet rounded corners. You can simply round off your corners, or you might want to try your hand at a scalloped or a wavy edge—giving your quilt a sentimental feeling.

1. Quilt as you like, then trim your edges using a template or by marking first with a fabric pencil, measuring along the length so your curves or scallops are evenly spaced.

2. Use bias binding for your curved edge, as you need the slight stretch that bias binding gives.

3. Pin the binding to the front of the quilt, matching the raw edge of the binding with the raw edge of the quilt, just a few lengths ahead of where you are sewing. As you sew, you will be easing it around the curves, but not stretching it.

4. When you need to adjust the quilt, pivot it rather than pulling at it.

5. When you reach the end, join the binding strips together with a 45-degree-angle seam.

6. When hand stitching the binding down onto the back of the quilt (or machine stitching onto the front of the quilt), stitch one curve at a time, stopping to ease the binding around the curves as you did on the top of the quilt.

ALTERNATIVE TO BINDING: FACING A QUILT

Facing is a neat alternative for finishing a quilt; it gives it a firm, invisible finish, creating a contemporary appearance or allowing you to add bunting, scallops, or prairie points to your quilt edge. Attaching a facing is similar to attaching binding; however, when folding it over to cover the edge, you take the whole of the binding toward the back, leaving the quilt at the front going right up to the edge (the facing is not seen from the front). Use binding made from the same material as your quilt back.

1. Sew to the quilt top as you would for your regular binding.

2. Press the seam open to ensure a neat edge.

3. Instead of folding over the binding to enclose the raw edge of the quilt, fold the entire binding over to the back, so that the seam line is right on the edge of the quilt. Press.

4. Pin into place and hand sew the back with a blind stitch to finish.

SIGNING AND LABELING QUILTS

It is important to label your quilt so others know who made it and when. Create a label, using a permanent marker, alphabet stamps and permanent ink, stencils, embroidery, or photo transfer fabric and then hand or machine appliqué the label onto the quilt backing. You can use fusible webbing to attach your label before sewing around the edges.

You can also directly sign your quilt in a corner somewhere on the front or back with permanent marker, either freehand, with a stencil, or with embroidery.

I recently saw a quilter who had had some fabric labels custom made at an online print-on-demand fabric shop. She designed her colorful labels with her logo, name, and some interesting graphics; uploaded it to the print-on-demand fabric Web site; and ordered some yardage. All she has to do is cut out one of the labels from her custom label fabric and appliqué it onto the back of her quilt or onto anything else she sews when she needs it. What a really clever idea.

APPLIQUÉ

Appliqué involves laying a shaped piece of fabric on top of a base fabric and stitching around the edges. There are a lot of different ways you can use appliqué, and there are several appliqué quilts in this book; some are made with a raw edge, others with the edge turned under. Most are machine stitched, but one very special quilt, Pop Wreath, is hand sewn.

METHOD 1:
FREEZER PAPER EDGES TURNED UNDER

I use freezer paper to create my appliqué motifs when I need the seams turned under. Trace your design template onto freezer paper (see page 27 for more about freezer paper) and iron it, wax side down, to the **Wrong** side of the fabric. This will hold it in place.

Cut around your shape, leaving a seam allowance. If the design is curved, snip the curves a little—not all the way to the seam line. With the tip of the iron, press the seam allowance over the freezer-paper template, working carefully, to hold it in place; if you have one, using a mini iron would be perfect here. If there are outer corners, fold the corner into the center, then fold the sides over to meet it; inner corners need to be clipped. Continue to press firmly with the hot iron, until you have a crisp edge all around. Remove the freezer paper before attaching your appliqué piece to your background fabric. Pin, or use a dab of appliqué glue, to hold the piece in place while you sew.

PERFECT APPLIQUÉ CIRCLES

Instead of time-consuming, careful snipping of curves and pressing, try this short-cut method: Iron your freezer-paper template onto the fabric and cut around leaving a ½-in/12-mm seam allowance; sew a long loose basting stitch with your sewing machine (or by hand) all the way around the circle, about halfway into the seam allowance. This will naturally gather the fabric and curve the seam allowance around the freezer paper. Press around to create a curved edge. No need to remove the stitches—just keep them there. Remove the freezer paper and attach your circle patch, using your preferred method.

METHOD 2:
NEEDLE TURN

Cut out your appliqué piece from fabric using a template and lay it onto the **Right** side of the background fabric, **Right** side up. When cutting, be sure to leave a seam allowance all around if your template does not include a seam allowance, and mark the edge of the seam line onto the **Right** side of the fabric with tailor's chalk or a water-soluble pen (test first to make sure it will come out later). Pin or baste your appliqué piece into place on your background fabric. As you sew, turn the edges under to the marked line, using your needle to push the seam under, and use a blind hemming stitch to sew in position.

METHOD 3:
RAW EDGE WITH DOUBLE-SIDED FUSIBLE WEBBING

Trace your template/motif designs onto the paper side of the fusible webbing, roughly cut out the webbing around the design, and place it with the sticky side down to the **Wrong** side of the fabric. Press into place with a hot iron and when it is cool, use a pair of small sharp scissors to cut carefully around the outline of the design. Peel back the paper; the sticky stuff should have adhered to the **Wrong** side of the fabric. Place your fabric motif, sticky side down, onto the **Right** side of your background fabric. Once you have all your motifs in place, press them into position. Machine sew around the edge using a zigzag stitch, straight stitch, or blanket stitch. Use a thread that matches your motif rather than your background.

BASIC HAND STITCHES

RUNNING STITCH

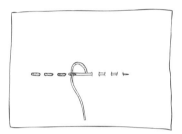

This simple stitch is used for quilting and creating decorative lines when one is embroidering. To create the running stitch, pass the needle in and out of the fabric, keeping both the stitch length and the length of the space in between equal. The basting stitch, used for keeping fabric in place while sewing, is similar but with very long stitches and spaces in between.

BLIND STITCH (ALSO KNOWN AS "SLIP STITCH")

If done properly, this stitch is almost invisible from both sides. It is often used for hemming, for appliqué, or to attach binding. In this version, the needle does not go through all the layers of fabric, resulting in a stitch that will not be seen on the other side.

Working from right to left, take a stitch in the folded edge, then take a tiny stitch in the fabric directly opposite where the needle came out; continue by slanting the needle under the fold and coming up again vertically.

LADDER STITCH

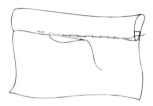

This stitch is easy and fast—perfect for hand sewing your binding. It's worked as a sort of off-center running stitch, and if done properly, is almost invisible on the top side of your work.

Working from right to left, take a running stitch parallel to your binding into the quilt fabric (do not go through to the back), then take another stitch into your binding edge, ensuring that your needle enters the fabric exactly above the area where it exited.

BLANKET STITCH

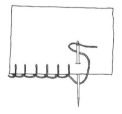

This stitch is used to reinforce edges and is very handy for attaching appliqué. Going from left to right, insert the needle in position in the upper line and take a straight downward stitch, keeping the thread under the point of the needle. Pull up the stitch to form a loop and repeat.

CARING FOR YOUR QUILT

Once you have finished making your quilt, you will want to display it, use it, or store it away.

DISPLAYING

Be sure the quilt is not in direct sunlight, since this will fade the fabrics.

Avoid areas near heating vents, fireplaces, and walls that may heat up in the summer sun. Moisture is also bad for textiles, so be careful not to hang quilts near evaporative coolers or humidifiers.

Wherever you hang it, you should change your quilt's location every six months in order to protect it.

When hanging your quilt, you must distribute the weight evenly so you don't put any stress on the seams or the fabric.

Never pierce a quilt with nails or use metal clips to hang it; this would damage the fabric.

To hang your quilt, attach a narrow sleeve to the back and hang with a dowel or curtain rod. This distributes the weight evenly and will not damage the quilt.

MAKE A HANGING SLEEVE

Measure the width of your quilt and cut a strip of cotton or muslin fabric that is 8 in/20 cm long and the same width as your quilt.

Hem the short edges by folding ¼ in/6 mm under and under again; pin and sew.

Fold the strip of fabric lengthwise, **Wrong** sides together, matching the raw edges, then sew along the raw edges with a ¼-in/6-mm seam allowance, making a tube.

Lay it out so the seam lies in the center of the tube and press it open. You won't turn it **Right** side out; instead, lay the open seam against the back of the quilt about ½ in/12 mm below where the binding finishes.

Blind stitch the top and bottom edges of the sleeve to the quilt back, making sure not to stitch through to the quilt front.

An alternative method for short-term quilt hanging that doesn't involve sewing or attaching anything to the quilt is to securely attach a strip of stainless steel to the wall, just the width of the quilt. Then use tiny rare-earth magnets all along the front of the quilt, attaching it to the stainless steel strip on the wall.

STORING

Store textiles in a dark, dry place like an airing cupboard or linen cupboard. Store them either rolled up or folded, and unfold and refold your quilts twice a year to prevent permanent creases from forming. If you are storing quilts for long periods or the quilts contain delicate or antique fabrics, wrap them in unbleached muslin or cotton before storing.

WASHING

It is generally fine to wash your machine-sewn and machine-quilted all-cotton quilts in your washing machine (although for a large quilt, you may need to make use of a commercial washing machine at your local laundromat). Use cold water and a mild detergent and use the gentle cycle. It's okay to put this sort of everyday quilt in the dryer, but don't iron your quilt—there's no need.

For hand-sewn quilts, quilts using wool batting, or quilts with delicate fabrics and embellishments, hand-wash using cold water and gentle detergent (the bathtub comes in handy for hand-washing large quilts) and line-dry out of direct sunlight (antique quilts should not be washed at all).

You don't need to wash your everyday quilt more than once a year unless very soiled. In between its annual wash you may like to air it outside occasionally and spot wash any staining.

When washing a quilt for the first time or washing a quilt with fabrics where the color might run, you might like to wash using a mild soap specifically made to remove any unfixed dye from fibers and to keep it from redepositing the dye onto other areas (there are several products on the market that do this job—ask at your local quilt shop).

CHARM
SQUARES

Charm Squares have traditionally been sized at 1-in/2.5-cm, 2½-in/6-cm, or 5-in/12-cm squares, and have been used for over a hundred years to make Charm quilts or Around the World quilts. Nowadays, Charm Square sizes have been standardized to make buying and selling them easier. These packs of pre-cut 5-in/12-cm squares contain a sample of each design from a single fabric collection, or are made up by quilt shops in color-coordinated packs. Charm Packs offer great variety without a big initial outlay in cost. You can use them to make simple traditional block designs and keep the leftovers for appliqué projects.

For one of the quilts in this book, I purchased scrap packs of hard to find Japanese fabrics (available on Etsy.com), and trimmed them down to make my own Charm Packs using a 5-in/12-cm square ruler. I've also used Robert Kaufman's Kona Solids, which I'm more than a little addicted to—they are just like packs of candy with 4 different tonal ranges (darks, pastels, brights, and classic), and are incredibly versatile. I recommend keeping a pack or two in your stash. I have also used the Moda's collections, Erin Michael's Lush, and French General's Rural Jardin. I am especially excited to showcase some delicious hand screen-printed cotton/linen from Australian independent fabric design group Ink & Spindle.

The following projects are included
in this chapter, all using Charm Squares:

ALOFT: *   **CLOUD SONG:** **   **SQUARE DANCE:** ***
COMMUNITY GARDEN: **   **CONSTRUCTIVIST:** **

ALOFT

A vintage postcard that used to hang in my studio inspired this quilt. Seeing a hot-air balloon in the sky never fails to awe me and my children—it is still high on our "to do" list to go for a ride someday! This design is a perfect way to use up your favorite fabric scraps, and it's so easy you could make a few of these for new-baby gifts.

Finished quilt size: 45 × 35 in/114 × 89 cm

DIFFICULTY LEVEL ✳ This baby crib quilt is very easy to put together; it involves simple sewing of squares and an easy introduction to appliqué.

FABRIC: 36 squares (5 in/12 cm) of Japanese linens and cottons, a pack of pre-cut Charm Squares (5 in/12 cm), or cut your own squares from pieces of your scraps

BACKGROUND: 1⅓ yd/1.2 m of 44-in-/112-cm-wide fabric of your choice to complement your Charm Squares (I used a cotton/linen in a subtle blue stripe)

BACKING: 1½ yd/1.4 m of 44-in-/112-cm-wide cotton or linen fabric of your choice (I used a sky blue solid cotton)

BATTING: 50-×-40-in/127-×-102-cm piece of batting. You might like to use wool batting as there is some hand quilting involved and wool batting makes this baby quilt so warm and snuggly; however, if you need an easy-care option for baby's bedding, use cotton batting, which can be washed easily.

BINDING: ½ yd/46 cm of fabric to match or complement your background fabric

THREAD: Off-white cotton thread suitable for piecing, and good-quality cotton machine quilting thread that will complement your quilt (I used a variegated blue, which adds a bit of extra texture and dimension to the cloud quilting design). Embroidery or hand-quilting thread, such as perle cotton, in various colors for the hand-quilted elements (I used a dark blue, medium teal, and red).

OTHER INGREDIENTS: Rotary cutter • mat • 5-in/12-cm ruler • hand-quilting or embroidery needle (depending on how small your stitches are and how chunky your thread is) • basting spray • hand-quilting hoop • thimble

---

NOTES

• Use ¼-in/6-mm seam allowances throughout.

PREPARING YOUR FABRIC

1. If you're using pre-cut Charm Squares, there is hardly any cutting at all; or cut 36 squares, each 5 in/12 cm, from fabric scraps.

2. Cut out a 45-×-35-in/114-×-89-cm piece of your background fabric.

MAKING THE QUILT TOP

1. Using ¼-in/6-mm seam allowances throughout, sew all of the Charm Squares together into one large 6-×-6 grid block of Charm Squares. Press seams open as you go, to reduce bulk for hand quilting. Press the piece flat, then cut out the balloon shape, per the layout diagram below.

2. Make the basket by sewing the leftover 2 bottom corners together (see diagram) and cut out the basket shape.

3. Lay out your background fabric on your work surface and lay the balloon and basket on a slight angle on the background fabric. Ensure they are at least 4 in/10 cm away from the outside edges. Once they are positioned, smooth them down all over with your hands, ensuring they are flat and wrinkle free. Press them in place with your iron; this will hold them temporarily. Lift up one half of the balloon and fold over, then spray lightly with basting spray. Lay this side back down and smooth over with your hands. Do the same thing with the other half and with the basket. Lift up the edges and spray a little of the basting spray under the edges that are not stuck down and again smooth over.

4. Leave the basting spray to dry for 10 minutes or it will gum up your needles and cause you to skip stitches. Take your quilt top to your sewing machine and, using the off-white thread, stitch around the outside of the balloon and basket with a zigzag or blanket stitch (the rest of the balloon will be held in position with quilting later). Your quilt top is now complete.

QUILTING AND FINISHING

For instructions on making the batting and backing, see pages 34 and 36.

1. Layer the quilt top with the batting and backing, and baste, using your preferred basting method (see page 37).

2. Using a thread that matches your background fabric or one to contrast (I used variegated blue), machine quilt with an all-over fill design (see page 40; I used a cloud design, which is perfect for this quilt). Quilt carefully up to and around the balloon and basket.

3. Using perle cotton and a simple, chunky running stitch (see page 48), hand quilt using the design suggested. Stitch in the balloon strings to hold up the basket, and stitch along the inside edges of the balloon and basket.

4. Following the instructions on page 43, make 175 in/ 445 cm of continuous straight-cut binding; cut strips 2½ in/ 6 cm wide. Press and attach the binding in your preferred method (see page 44).

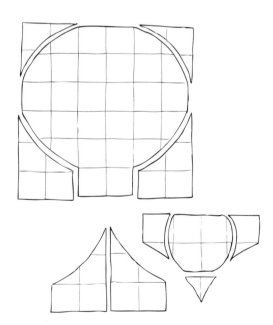

CLOUD SONG

As a child, I loved drawing and gazing at clouds. I designed this toddler quilt, with its colorful squares and cartoon-like clouds, to bring some child-like dreaminess into your life. With its bright colors and hand-drawn motifs, this quilt is easy to personalize; feel free to draw your own cloud design or use your children's drawings as inspiration. Use the finished quilt as a crib quilt, floor play mat, or nursing lap quilt.

Finished quilt size: 54 in/137 cm square

DIFFICULTY LEVEL ✹✹

This quilt is pretty easy to put together. The Charm Square blocks can be made using the chain-piecing method (see page 32). While cutting out the shapes for the appliqué may take a few extra minutes, using fusible webbing (see note below) and raw edge machine appliqué means that this quilt can come together in less than a day.

FABRIC: 2 packs of solid-color Charm Squares (5 in/12 cm); 48 squares for the blocks and 15 extra squares in bright colors to make the raindrops

BACKGROUND: 1½ yd/1.4 m of 44-in-/112-cm-wide fabric for the alternate squares (I used a soft pastel stripe, but any light-colored fabric would work)

CLOUDS: ½ yd/46 cm of 44-in-/112-cm-wide white textured fabric

BACKING: 3½ yd/3.2 m of 44-in-/112-cm-wide cotton fabric (I used 2 different pieces of striped fabric)

BATTING: 60-in-/147-cm-square piece of cotton batting

BINDING: ½ yd/46 cm of 44-in/112-cm-wide cotton fabric

THREAD: Neutral-color cotton thread suitable for piecing and quilting, plus thread in various colors to match your Charm Squares

OTHER INGREDIENTS: Rotary cutter • mat • ruler • fusible webbing or basting spray • iron • small, sharp scissors

TEMPLATE: 4 cloud appliqué pieces and raindrop template in template envelope (enough for your appliqué pieces—1 to 2 yd/0.9 to 1.8 m depending upon width)

NOTES

• Use ¼-in/6-mm seam allowances throughout.

• Pieced block measures 18½ in/47 cm; finished block size is 18 in/46 cm.

• Depending on what sort of textured fabric you're using for the clouds, fusible webbing may or may not be appropriate. If using a cotton or linen woven fabric such as the pleated cotton shown, fusible webbing will work fine; if using a chenille or terry cloth (both excellent ideas), use a basting spray to hold your clouds in place while you sew around their edges.

PREPARING YOUR FABRIC

1. Cut 5 squares (each 18½ in/47 cm) from your background fabric (plain blocks).

2. Make 28 to 29 raindrops: Choose 15 Charm Squares in a combination of the brightest colors. (Two raindrops can be cut from each Charm Square. Trace the raindrop template onto fusible webbing [see page 28] and roughly cut around them in pairs.) Place them, sticky side down, onto the **Wrong** side of the Charm Squares; press with a hot iron until fused. Cut out carefully, using small, sharp scissors. I cut about 28 raindrops; you might want to allow extra to mix and match.

3. Trace the 4 cloud shape templates (or draw your own freehand) onto fusible webbing. Roughly cut out the shapes and place them, sticky side down, onto the **Wrong** side of your cloud fabric. Use a hot iron to fuse the webbing in place, then carefully cut around each cloud using small, sharp scissors. (See Notes on page 59: If fusible webbing will not work on the cloud fabric chosen, trace or draw shapes on the **Wrong** side of the fabric and cut out.)

MAKING THE QUILT TOP

1. Sew 48 Charm Squares (16 squares for each pieced block) into 4 blocks of a 4-×-4 grid, each pieced block measuring 18½ in/47 cm square.

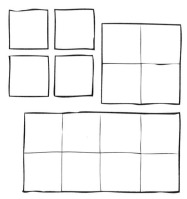

2. Lay the clouds on pieced Charm Square blocks; press into position with a hot iron or attach with basting spray. Using white thread, machine sew around the edges of the clouds, with a zigzag or blanket stitch.

3. Lay 5 to 6 raindrops, sticky side down, on each plain block; press into place with a hot iron. Using thread to match the color of your raindrops, machine sew around the edge of each raindrop with a zigzag or blanket stitch.

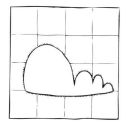

4. Lay out the completed blocks as per the layout diagram, sew in rows, and press the seams to one side. Pin rows together, matching seams, before sewing. The quilt top is now complete.

QUILTING AND FINISHING

For instructions on making the batting and backing, see pages 34 and 36.

1. Layer the quilt top with batting and backing, and baste, using your preferred basting method (see page 37).

2. Using a neutral-color thread, machine quilt with a free-motion cloud design (see page 40), going up to and around the raindrops and clouds.

3. Following the instructions on page 43, make 230 in/ 584 cm of continuous bias-cut binding; cut the strips 2½ in/ 6 cm wide. Press and attach the binding in your preferred method (see page 44). Here I finished it with soft rounded corners (hence the need for bias binding).

SQUARE DANCE

This traditional Central Medallion quilt is made with several packs of Charm Squares. Having all of the squares pre-cut means that this quilt, despite its size, comes together quickly. It is a romantic-style quilt and meant for a large bed, making it a lovely centerpiece for any room. I used a French country–inspired fabric collection, but any reproduction prints will work just as well.

__Finished quilt size:__ 108 in/274 cm square—perfect for a generous queen- or king-size bed

DIFFICULTY LEVEL ✱✱✱  This quilt is made by chain piecing (see page 32) Charm Squares and introduces triangle piecing. Advanced quilters might like to challenge themselves with the tight stipple quilting on the central square and diamond. The curved edge adds a touch of whimsy to this otherwise geometric design.

FABRIC: 288 Charm Squares (5 in/12 cm)—7 packs of 42 squares (or cut your own squares from a total of 5½ yd/5 m, choosing a range with a romantic mix of floral or reproduction prints)

BORDERS: 3¾ yd/3.4 m of 44-in-/112-cm-wide off-white cotton and 3½ yd/3.2 m of a 44-in-/112-cm-wide coordinating solid fabric (I used a smoky blue)

BACKING: 9½ yd/8.7 m of 44-in-/112-cm-wide cotton fabric in a coordinating print; if using extra-wide 120-in/305-cm backing fabric, you will need 3 yd/2.7 m

BATTING: 115-in-/290-cm-square piece of cotton batting

BINDING: 1 yd/0.9 m of 44-in-/112-cm-wide fabric. You will need to make bias binding (see page 42) to bind around the curved edge; use a coordinating fabric, such as one of the plain colors or one of the prints.

THREAD: Neutral-color cotton thread suitable for piecing and machine quilting

OTHER INGREDIENTS: Rotary cutter • mat • ruler • 5-in-/12-cm square quilting ruler (optional) • scissors • tailor's chalk • pins • iron

---

NOTES

- Use ¼-in/6-mm seam allowances throughout.
- Two different blocks are used in this quilt—the Charm Square block and the triangle block. You will need 32 triangle blocks.
- When sewing together the print Charm Squares, take them at random from the packs, making sure that there is a nice mix of tone and pattern throughout.

PREPARING YOUR FABRIC

1. If not using pre-cut Charm Squares, cut 288 squares (each 5 in/12 cm), from print fabric of choice. You can do this easily with a rotary cutter, mat, and a 5-in-/12-cm-wide ruler.

2. Cut 48 squares (each 5 in/12 cm) from the off-white fabric.

3. You can cut the border strips along the length of the fabric to avoid having any joins; be sure that the length of fabric purchased is as long as the longest piece needed, but do NOT cut these until you are ready with the actual measurements of the pieced center panel. (See Completing the Quilt Top instructions as to when you should cut these strips.) Cutting the strips lengthwise on the fabric makes for stronger borders, as they are cut along the warp of the fabric rather than the weft.

MAKING THE QUILT TOP

1. *Triangle blocks:* Place 32 white squares on top of 32 print Charm Squares, **Right** sides facing. With a ruler, draw a line from the top right corner to the bottom left corner, and pin them together; do this for each pair of squares. Chain piece all squares with the sewing machine, sewing directly on the drawn line. Cut the blocks, leaving a ¼-in/6-mm seam allowance along the sewn edge. Open up the blocks and press; triangle blocks measure 5 in/12 cm square.

> **Tip:** If you can't stand to waste the smaller leftover pieces, sew an additional ½ in/12 mm to one side of your drawn line when chain piecing the squares, before separating and cutting. Then, when cutting, simply cut half way between the two sewn lines leaving a ¼-in/6-mm seam allowance on both. The larger triangle block is used for this quilt—the smaller block can be used to make up matching cushion covers.

2. *Center panel:* Keep your layout diagram close by and take note of where the triangle half white blocks are placed and in which direction they are facing when sewing them into the rows. Following the diagram, lay out your print and white Charm Squares and triangle pieced blocks;

sew together in groups of ten, one row at a time—you will use the remaining 16 solid white Charm Squares for the diamond in the center panel. Starting with the top row

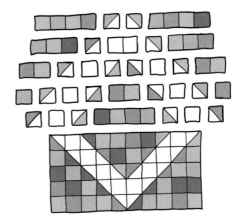

of the center panel, sew rows together, pressing seams in a different direction on every alternate row.

3. When you have completed the center panel, press and measure the sides to ensure you're on track—it should measure 45½ in/116 cm square.

COMPLETING THE QUILT TOP

1. Cut 2 strips from the solid-color fabric, 10 in/25 cm wide and the same length (45½ in/116 cm) as the center panel (measure to be sure). Pin and sew these strips onto the top and bottom of your square, and press seams to one side.

2. Measure the sides of your panel, including the top and bottom strips added in step 1; these should now measure 64½ in/164 cm. From solid-color fabric, cut two strips 10 in/25 cm wide and the same length as the sides; pin and sew these onto the sides of the center panel. Press seams to one side, and then press this entire piece.

3. Chain piece 136 print Charm Squares into pairs. Press seams to one side. Sew the remaining squares onto these pairs to make blocks of 3 squares. Press seams.

4. Sew 2 of the blocks together, making a 2-x-3 block. Continue sewing 3 square blocks together, making 2 strips, each 3-×-20 Charm Squares long and two strips 3-×-14 Charm Squares long. Press all seams.

5. Attach the 14 Charm Square strips to the top and to the bottom of the center panel (some careful pinning will help with this) pinning at each seam; then sew and press. Attach the 20 Charm Square strips to each side of the center panel (again, pinning carefully to ensure it fits well along the length of the center quilt panel). Press seams to one side, then press the entire panel. After you have pressed this larger panel, measure the sides; they should be 90½ in/230 cm.

6. Cut 2 strips, 90½ × 5 in/230 × 12 cm, from off-white fabric. Check the measurement against your quilted piece and join these to the top and bottom of your pieced panel. Next, cut 2 strips, 99½ × 5 in/253 × 12 cm from off-white fabric (again, measure the panel to check), and sew to each side of the pieced panel, pinning at regular intervals. Press seams to one side.

7. Follow the above procedure for the final border. The strips should measure 99½ × 5 in/253 × 12 cm and 109 × 5 in/ 277 × 12 cm respectively, but again measure the quilt to check. Sew and press.

Tip: If you don't want your quilt to be quite this big, leave off the two outer borders. If you decide to do this, don't include a curved edge, so as not to cut into your Charm Squares.

QUILTING AND FINISHING

For instructions on making the batting and backing, see pages 34 and 36.

1. Layer the quilt top with batting and backing, and baste, using your preferred basting method (see page 37).

2. Using a neutral-color quilting thread, machine quilt the solid-color square and diamond with a very tight stipple quilting design (see page 40). This will give the center area definition. Quilt the remaining areas using a larger stipple design.

3. Lay your quilt out somewhere flat and large. Using tailor's chalk, draw a wavy line from the outside of the colored band to the inside of the off-white band—leaving an inch to spare on either side, and trimming the blue entirely from the corners. Make the wavy lines approximately 3 Charm Squares long; when you get to the corners, make sure they are symmetrical. Use the layout diagram as a guide. Once you're satisfied that your wavy line is even and symmetrical, cut along your line with scissors. No turning back once you have started, so cut without fear but with caution.

4. Following the instructions on page 43, make 13 yd/12 m of continuous bias-cut binding; cut strips 2½ in/6 cm wide. Press and attach the binding using your preferred method; see page 45 for tips on attaching binding to curved edges.

COMMUNITY GARDEN

This design was inspired by our vegetable garden and local community gardens. Community gardens are amazing places, where people can help each other, the community, and the environment and work toward a healthier lifestyle. This couch throw, wall hanging, or even crib quilt, is made from the most gorgeous hand-printed fabric. The fact that this fabric has ecofriendly properties and earthy textures adds to the community spirit.

Finished quilt size: 41 in/104 cm square

DIFFICULTY LEVEL ✱✱ This quilt introduces curved piecing in an otherwise simple 9-patch design.

FABRIC: 72 pre-cut Charm Squares (5 in/12 cm)—2 or 3 packs, depending on how many squares are in each pack (I made my own, using small packs of Ink and Spindle boutique fabric, in a linen cotton blend)

BACKGROUND: ⅜ yd/35 cm of 44-in-/112-cm-wide tan or off-white linen blend fabric

CENTER PIECE: 1 Fat Quarter (18 × 22 in/46 × 56 cm) of your favorite fabric

BACKING: 1⅓ yd / 1.2 m of 44-in-/112-cm-wide linen

BATTING: 46-in-/110-cm-square piece of cotton batting

BINDING: ⅜ yd/35 cm of 44-in-/112-cm-wide coordinating fabric

THREAD: Neutral-color cotton thread suitable for piecing and machine quilting

OTHER INGREDIENTS: Rotary cutter • mat • ruler • 5-in/12-cm square quilting ruler (optional) • scissors • tailor's chalk

TEMPLATE: Pattern pieces for block

NOTES

- Use ¼-in/6-mm seam allowances throughout.
- Pieced block measures 14 in/35.5 cm square; finished block size is 13½ in/34 cm square.
- Press seams open as you go; because the fabric is heavy, this will reduce bulkiness.

PREPARING YOUR FABRIC

1. If you are preparing your own Charm Squares, you will need to cut out 72 squares, each 5 in/12 cm.

2. Using the template, cut 36 of the outside curve pattern pieces from the background fabric.

MAKING THE QUILT TOP

1. Sew a 9-patch block (3 rows of 3 squares) using 9 different colored/patterned Charm Squares—you will need to make 8 of these 9-patch blocks.

2. Trim the Fat Quarter to the same size as the 9-patch blocks (14 in/35.5 cm square) for the center panel.

3. Lay the inside curve pattern piece template onto the outside corners of each 9-patch block and the corners of the center panel piece, with the curve facing out. Draw a chalk line along the template and trim to the line. (See page 34 for more help on piecing curves.)

4. Fold the outside curve pieces, which were cut from the background fabric, in half and finger press, marking the center. Fold the corner curves on the 9-patch blocks and center piece, and finger press, marking the center. Match up these center lines on both curves of one corner and place a pin at the center point, then continue carefully pinning together the right sides of the convex and concave curves. Sew, using a ¼-in/6-mm seam allowance. Do this for all remaining corners, then press a seam allowance in the direction in which the curve naturally falls.

5. Trim any loose bits. Lay the blocks out on a flat surface and arrange the pieced blocks around the central panel. Sew the blocks together, first into rows and then sew the rows together, matching up the seams. Press the seam allowance on each row in alternate directions. Press the entire quilt top flat.

QUILTING AND FINISHING

For instructions on making the batting and backing, see pages 34 and 36.

1. Layer the quilt top with batting and backing, and baste, using your preferred basting method (see page 37).

2. Using a neutral-color thread, machine quilt with a large modern leaf design (see page 40), as I used, to echo the fabric, or use a simple stipple.

3. Following the instructions on page 43, make 180 in/ 457 cm of continuous straight-cut binding; cut strips 2½ in/ 6 cm wide. Press and attach the binding in your preferred method (see page 44).

4. If you are planning on using this as a wall hanging, you will need to make and attach a hanging sleeve to the back, using the instructions on page 50. Your quilt is now finished.

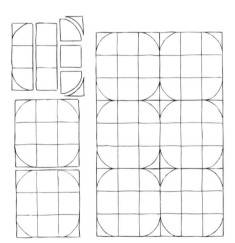

CONSTRUCTIVIST

My children used to have a set of simple wooden blocks painted in bright colors. They would build up towers and knock them down again, over and over. Every time the tower fell, we'd hear their joyful high-pitched squeals. This quilt is inspired by those blocks and is for all curious folks who find happiness in the smallest of places.

Finished quilt size: 36 × 50 in/91 × 127 cm

DIFFICULTY LEVEL ✱✱  This small quilt is a nice introduction to working with triangles and can be all rotary cut to make your life a whole lot easier.

FABRIC: 1 pack of pre-cut Charm Squares (5-in/12-cm) (I used Lush by Erin Michael for Moda, but any tonally neutral fabric would work)

BACKGROUND: 1⅓ yd/1.2 m of 44-in-/112-cm-wide cotton fabric (I used a khaki-color fabric, but a dark grey would also work well)

BACKING: 1½ yd/1.4 m of 44-in-/112-cm-wide fabric in coordinating colors (I pieced this with several leftover scraps and coordinating solid fabric)

BATTING: 41-×-55 in/104-×-140-cm piece of cotton batting

BINDING: ⅜ yd/35 cm of 44-in-/112-cm-wide coordinating fabric

THREAD: Neutral-color cotton thread suitable for piecing and variegated thread for machine quilting

OTHER INGREDIENTS: Rotary cutter • mat • ruler

TEMPLATE: Triangle pattern pieces

NOTES
• Use ¼-in/6-mm seam allowances throughout.

PREPARING YOUR FABRIC

1. Using the rotary cutter, mat, and ruler, cut 36 Charm Squares into full-size triangle shapes (C), using the template provided.

2. Cut 3 full-size triangle shapes (C) from your background fabric.

3. Cut 14 right-angle triangle shapes (A/B) from your background fabric, using the templates provided.

4. Cut from your background fabric:

- 2 strips, 9½ × 36 in/25 × 91 cm
- 1 strip, 22½ × 5 in/57 × 12 cm
- 2 strips, 17½ × 5 in/44 × 12 cm
- 1 strip, 15 × 5 in/38 × 12 cm
- 3 strips, 12½ × 5 in/32 × 12 cm
- 2 strips, 10 × 5 in/25 × 12 cm
- 3 strips, 7½ × 5 in/19 × 12 cm
- 2 pieces, 5 in/12 cm square

MAKING THE QUILT TOP

1. Following the layout diagram, lay out your pieces—triangles, half triangles, and strips—on a clean table or your design wall.

2. Attach each row of triangles by first pinning each triangle to the next one and then sewing, using accurate seam allowances; press seams to one side. Press each piece without stretching the triangles out of shape, and trim the dog-ears from the corners.

3. Once you have sewn together the triangles in each row, sew your strip of fabric to both sides, using the layout diagram as a guide, and press again.

4. Pin the rows together, starting with the top and going down; pin carefully as you go, matching seams so that the triangles stay aligned. Sew and then press the entire quilt.

QUILTING AND FINISHING

For instructions on making the batting and backing, see pages 34 and 36.

1. Layer the quilt top with batting and backing, and baste using your preferred method (see page 37).

2. Using a neutral-color thread (I used a variegated thread), machine quilt with a wood-grain free-motion quilting design (see page 40) or your own preferred design.

3. Following the instructions on page 43, make 190 in/ 483 cm of continuous straight-cut binding; cut strips 2½-in/ 6 cm wide. Press and attach the binding in your preferred method (see page 44).

4. If you're planning on using this as a wall hanging, you will need to make and attach a hanging sleeve to the back, using the instructions on page 50. Your quilt is now finished.

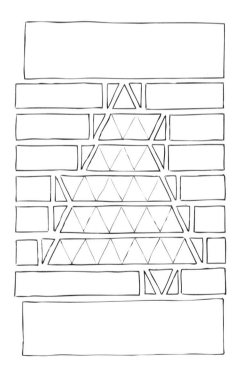

The following projects are included in this chapter, all using Jelly Roll Strips:

STEP LIVELY: **   **ELECTRIC SPECTRUM:** **

SQUADRON: ***   **RHOMBUS:** ***

LOLLYPOP TREE: **

JELLY ROLL STRIPS

Moda fabrics coined the term "Jelly Rolls," which refers to pre-cut 2½-in/6-cm strips of fabric, cut selvage to selvage, with pieces from an entire fabric range rolled up in a cute little "jelly roll" package. Depending on the manufacturer, you can expect about 40 strips in each color-coordinated pack. The strips are perfect for coin quilts and strip quilts, for using in between blocks as sashing, and as binding strips. Plus, being able to see and touch each piece of fabric in a single collection—before ordering yards and yards online—is very helpful.

Many fabric companies now stock or produce these roll-up strips, and they can vary in quantity and width: Moda's Jelly Rolls, Hoffman's Batik, Bali Pops, Island Batiks, Strip-Tease Buns, and Robert Kaufman's Kona Cotton Solids Roll Ups all contain the standard 40 strips of 44 x 2½ in/112 x 6 cm. Lecien's Sushi Rolls include 45 strips of 2⅞ in/7.3 cm; Windham Fabrics Fat Roll includes 19 strips of 44 x 5 in/112 x 12 cm; and Free Spirit's Design Rolls include 26 strips of 2½ in/6 cm. Moda also has a Honey Bun roll, which has strips that are 1½ in/4 cm wide.

When making the quilts in this chapter, if you don't have any pre-cut strips on hand but want to get sewing straight away, you can easily cut them from your stash. Simply cut 2½-in/6-cm strips, selvage to selvage, from your yardage. Or join shorter pieces using the method described in making continuous binding (see page 43). If you have a 2½-in/6-cm ruler, a cutting mat, and a rotary cutter, cutting your own strips is fairly easy. However, using a Jelly Roll pack will not only save you a couple of hours but also save your wrists. (If using a rotary cutter for any length of time, take a moment every 5 minutes to stretch your arms, back, and wrists.)

I used some delicious pre-cut strips in this section. Moda's white Basics are a must-have to keep in your stash and team up brilliantly with Robert Kaufman's Kona Solids and Moda's super-bright Marbles range. I also used a mixed floral range from Lecien; Tula Pink's Plume range; and Bar Harbor by Minick and Simpson for Moda.

STEP LIVELY

This strip quilt is made using a simple Bargello quilt technique, where you sew strips into loops, adjust their position to create your design, then cut the loops open at one end to reveal the fullness of your genius. This color gradient is a little tricky to get right and has a lot of strip piecing, but don't be daunted—it's fun to make. Get comfy before you get sewing. You are going to love this design!

Finished quilt size: 76½ × 80 in/194 × 221 cm— perfect for a teenager's bed or wall hanging

DIFFICULTY LEVEL **✱✱** This quilt offers an introduction to strip piecing and a simple Bargello-style quilt method.

FABRIC: 1 pack of mixed solid-color strips (I used Robert Kaufman's Kona solids in the classic palette)

1 Jelly Roll pack of basic white, or 2½ yd/2.3 m of white fabric cut into 2½-in/6-cm strips

BACKING: 5 yd/4.5 m of 44-in-/112-cm-wide fabric (bright, patterned, cotton fabric was used on this quilt)

BATTING: 81½-×-85-in/207-×-216-cm piece of cotton batting

BINDING: ¾ yd/70 cm of 44-in-/112-cm-wide fabric (we used white binding), or you can join 8 Jelly Roll strips to make your double-fold binding

THREAD: white or neutral-color cotton thread suitable for piecing and machine quilting

OTHER INGREDIENTS: Scissors • pencil • small scrap of cardboard • iron • water-soluble fabric pen • ruler

---

NOTES

- Use ¼-in/6-mm seam allowances throughout.

- As you're using pre-cuts, there is very minimal cutting involved—couldn't be any easier than this.

- There are 38 strips of colored fabric and 38 strips of white used in this quilt. Any leftover strips can be used for binding or for another project.

- This quilt involves a lot of straight sewing; you will want to have a few bobbins filled, and remember to stretch your back at regular intervals.

PREPARING YOUR FABRIC

1. Unravel your Jelly Rolls and give them a good shake outside—this will free up the dust that is sure to come out of them.

2. Remove any unwanted colors—I took out the browns and whites to be left with 38 strips; you can have less or more strips, as per your preference.

3. Trim off the selvages from the fabric strips.

MAKING THE QUILT TOP

1. Take one colored strip and one white strip, and sew them end-to-end, creating a big fabric loop. Press the seam open. Do this for all of the strips.

2. Lay out your sewn loops where you can see them all at once, in a color gradient, using the photograph as a guide. Start with the reds, oranges, and yellows; move on to the lighter greens through to the darker greens and turquoises; then on to the blues and purples; ending with pink and grey.

3. Make a small template out of cardboard, 2½ × 4 in/6 × 10 cm, to help with your offset. Start at the top row, and offset each line by approximately 4 in/10 cm.

4. Once you have offset all of the rows and are happy with the result, use your hot iron to press a crease all the way down the right side of the looped rows without moving any of the loops out of their position. Take your scissors and cut each row on the crease. Open out the looped rows to their full length.

5. Using a water-soluble fabric pen, number each row in sequential order to prevent messing up your design. Pin your strips along their length at regular intervals, pinning a few together at a time. Take these to the sewing machine, and sew together in sections of 10 or so. Doing it this way makes handling the quilt at the sewing machine a little easier. When you have sewn all the rows to complete your quilt top, press the entire quilt. If necessary, square up the quilt corners and sides.

QUILTING AND FINISHING

For instructions on making the batting and backing, see pages 34 and 36.

1. Layer the quilt top with batting and backing, and baste, using your preferred basting method (see page 37).

2. Using a white thread so that the quilting design will stand out against the solid rainbow colors, machine quilt with an all-over stipple design (see page 40). I used a long stipple—an enjoyable design to quilt.

3. Following the instructions on page 43, make 340 in/ 834 cm continuous straight-cut binding; cut strips 2½ in/ 6 cm wide. Press and attach the binding in your preferred method (see page 44).

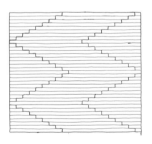
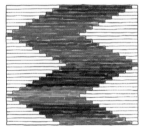

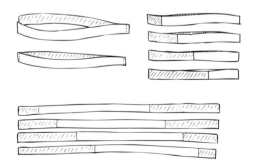

ELECTRIC SPECTRUM

This off-center lightning variation of a classic log cabin quilt is electrifying with its bright marble colors and white contrast. The brighter and more outrageous the fabric, the better. I used a pre-cut roll of vivid marble fabrics; however, you could quite easily use any crazily clashing colors, including fabrics from your scraps. Be sure to include hot pinks, sunny yellows, and acid greens in your mix.

Finished quilt size: 64½ × 80½ in/164 × 204 cm—perfect for a single bed

DIFFICULTY LEVEL ✱✱ If you prepare all your pieces beforehand, you can chain piece and make the blocks up assembly-line style. This quilt comes together quickly and if you use a quick binding method, you will likely be able to make it in a weekend.

FABRIC: 1 Jelly Roll pack of bright solids or marbles (I used Moda Marbles), or a total of 2½ yd/2.3 m of different bright fabrics cut into 2½-in/6-cm strips

1 Jelly Roll pack of white basics, or 2½ yd/2.3 m of white fabric cut into 2½-in/6-cm strips

BACKING: 5 yd/4.6 m of 44-in-/112-cm-wide fabric (I made a backing from vintage fabrics and solid strips using the system described on page 36 for an improvised scrappy backing, which makes a great alternate quilt on the other side)

BATTING: 70-×-85-in/178-×-216-cm piece of cotton batting

BINDING: ¾ yd/70 cm of 44-in-/112-cm-wide fabric, or use 8 Jelly Roll strips to make your binding

THREAD: White or neutral-color cotton thread suitable for piecing and quilting

OTHER INGREDIENTS: Rotary cutter • mat • ruler • iron • pins

NOTES
- Use ¼-in/6-mm seam allowances throughout.
- Trim block to measure 16½ in/42 cm square; finished block size is 16 in/41 cm square.

PREPARING YOUR FABRIC

1. Cut the following lengths from the white Jelly Roll strips. Set each size aside in a separate pile, ready to chain piece. To ensure you have an even amount of each color for each size, start by cutting the larger lengths first:

- 40 strips, 4½ in/11.5 cm
- 20 strips, 6½ in/16.5 cm
- 20 strips, 8½ in/21.5 cm
- 20 strips, 10½ in/26.5 cm
- 20 strips, 12¼ in/31 cm
- 20 strips, 14¼ in/36 cm

2. Cut the following lengths from the marbles Jelly Roll strips. Set each size aside in a separate pile, ready to chain piece. To ensure you have an even amount of each color for each size, start by cutting the larger lengths first:

- 20 strips, 4½ in/11 cm
- 20 strips, 6½ in/16.5 cm
- 20 strips, 8½ in/21.5 cm
- 20 strips, 10½ in/26.5 cm
- 20 strips, 12¼ in/31 cm
- 20 strips, 14¼ in/36 cm
- 20 strips, 16¼ in/41 cm

MAKING THE QUILT TOP

1. Center of blocks: With **Right** sides together, place one 4½-in/11-cm white strip together with the same size bright piece. Using the chain-piecing method (see page 32), sew along one long edge. Make 20 of these pairs. Press seams to one side. Continue sewing the strips until the blocks are complete.

2. Lay the blocks out on a clean surface or your design wall, as per the layout diagram. Sew the blocks together in rows. Press the seams of each alternate row in the opposite direction. Pin the rows at regular intervals to ensure the blocks line up, then sew together the rows.

QUILTING AND FINISHING

For instructions on making the batting and backing, see pages 34 and 36.

1. Layer the quilt top with batting and backing, and baste, using your preferred basting method (see page 37).

2. Using a white or colored thread (I used mauve for kicks), machine quilt with an all-over stipple design (see page 40). I used a long stipple variation to emphasize the strips.

3. Following the instructions on page 43, make 300 in/762 cm of continuous straight-cut binding; cut strips 2½ in/6 cm wide. Press and attach the binding in your preferred method (see page 44).

SQUADRON

As a child, I loved watching planes fly in formation and still do. Kids, especially boys, are fascinated with planes, so when I was designing a quilt especially for a boy, I knew I had to include an airplane block. While I was juggling the blocks around this way and that, I realized that I could make them fly in different formations, creating interesting geometric designs.

Finished quilt size: 57½ × 76½ in/146 × 194 cm

DIFFICULTY LEVEL ✱✱✱

This improvised-style strip-pieced airplane block is made using a cutting and piecing recipe, rather than a strict block pattern, and uses pre-cut strips to make your life easier. Don't fret about making each block exactly the same; allowing the blocks to be slightly off alignment adds to the charm of this quilt.

FABRIC: 1 Jelly Roll pack or 2 yd/1.8 m of red and blue fabrics cut into 2½-in/6-cm strips; choose a range of predominantly blues and reds and not too many florals (I used Bar Harbor by Minick and Simpson for Moda Fabrics)

BACKGROUND: 4 ⅓ yd/4 m of 44-in-/112-cm-wide solid-color cotton fabric (I used unbleached muslin)

BACKING: 3¾ yd/3.4 m of 44-in-/112-cm-wide fabric (I used unbleached muslin with 3 Fat Quarters to match the Jelly Roll fabrics)

BATTING: 65-×-82-in/165-×-208-cm piece of cotton batting

BINDING: ½ yd/46 cm of 44-in-/12-cm-wide cotton fabric (use a scrappy binding from leftover Jelly Roll strips)

THREAD: Neutral-color cotton thread suitable for piecing and quilting

OTHER INGREDIENTS: Rotary cutter • cutting mat • 10-in/25-cm square ruler • 5-in/12-cm square ruler

NOTES

- Use ¼-in/6-mm seam allowances throughout.
- Trim blocks to 10 in/25 cm square, to create a finished block size of 9½ in/24 cm square.

PREPARING YOUR FABRIC

1. Cut 48 squares from background fabric, each 10 in/ 25 cm; set aside 20 of these blocks, as they will not be cut.

2. Cut 10 squares from the background fabric, each 5 in/ 12 cm, then cut these squares in half, on the diagonal, to make 20 triangles.

3. Separate out 10 red/white strips from the Jelly Roll pack and set aside for the main plane body; separate out 20 blues/blacks from the Jelly Roll pack and set aside for the wings and tail.

MAKING UP THE BLOCKS

1. Cut 28 of the 10-in/25-cm background squares in half on the diagonal, forming 2 triangles from each. Sew in a red strip, corner to corner, **Right** sides together; this forms the plane body. Press seams toward outside edges.

2. Cut each block in half again, on the opposite diagonal (across the body of the plane). Sew in a blue strip, corner to corner, **Right** sides together, sewing half of the square to each side of the blue strip. Press seams toward outside edges. Trim 1 in/2.5 cm from one side of the remaining blue strips; you will have one pile of 1-in-/2.5-cm-wide strips and one pile of 1½-in-/4-cm-wide strips.

3. On each block, make another cut, parallel to and 2 in/ 5 cm away from the plane wing (blue strip). Sew in a 1½-in/ 4-cm strip. Reattach the other piece—ensuring it is centered. Press.

4. On the other side of each square, make another cut, near the tail of the plane, parallel to and 4 in/10 cm away from the main wing. Sew in a 1-in/2.5-cm strip, but instead of reattaching the other section, discard the piece and replace it with one of the triangle cuts from the background fabric. Press.

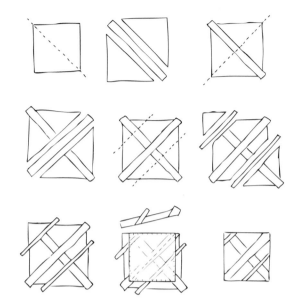

5. Press each block flat. Place the 10-in/25-cm square ruler over each square, one at a time, and line up the center diagonal line with the main plane wing and ensure that the corners are aligned. Using the rotary cutter, trim each block to 10 in/25 cm square.

COMPLETING THE QUILT TOP

1. Arrange the airplane blocks and the plain blocks in the order shown in the layout diagram, turning the airplane blocks around as required to achieve the formation in the diagram.

2. Sew pieced blocks together in pairs, then in blocks of four (2-×-2 grid), then sew the 2-×-2 blocks together, making sure that the corners match up. Because the blocks were made with a recipe rather than a strict pattern, some of the plane wings may not align perfectly; don't worry. As an improvised block, this a natural outcome.

3. Once all the blocks have been sewn together to complete your quilt top, press the seams to one side, and press the top flat.

QUILTING AND FINISHING

For instructions on making the batting and backing, see pages 34 and 36.

1. Layer the quilt top with batting and backing, and baste, using your preferred basting method (see page 37).

2. Using a neutral-color thread, machine quilt with a geometric design (see page 40).

3. Following the instructions on page 43 to make 300 in/ 762 cm of continuous straight-cut binding; cut strips 2½ in/ 6 cm wide. Press and attach the binding in your preferred method (see page 44).

RHOMBUS

This strip quilt is based on an old favorite Amish design sometimes known as Roman Stripes (or just Stripes). Naturally, the Amish only use solid fabrics, but here I have chosen a Jelly Roll with a good mix of lights and darks, to allow contrast. The black border sets off this design. When I was trying to think of a name for this quilt, I was stuck on diamonds, but as I described the project to my clever husband, he thought the shape sounded like a rhombus: a 4-sided shape where all the sides are of equal lengths.

Finished quilt size: 69½ in/177 cm square

DIFFICULTY LEVEL ✳✳✳ This quilt offers an easy introduction to foundation piecing.

FABRIC: 1 Jelly Roll; choose a range with good contrast (I used Plume by Tula Pink for Moda)

BORDER: 2¾ yd/2.5 m of a 44-in-/112-cm-wide contrasting fabric (I used a prewashed black textured silk fabric to make the central blocks stand out)

BACKING: 4⅓ yd/4 meters of a 44-in-/112-cm-wide complementary fabric

BATTING: 75-in-/191-cm-square piece of cotton batting

BINDING: ¾ yd/70 cm of fabric to match your border fabric

THREAD: Neutral-color cotton thread suitable for piecing and machine quilting

OTHER INGREDIENTS: Rotary cutter • mat • quilting ruler • craft paper for your foundation squares • pencil • sewing machine needle for sewing through paper only • appliqué glue • iron • pins

TEMPLATE: Foundation block pattern

NOTES

• Use ¼-in/6-mm seam allowances throughout.

• Sew this in production-line style.

• Trim your block to 12 in/30.5 cm; finished block size is 11½ in/29 cm.

PREPARING YOUR FABRIC

1. Sort your pre-cut strips into 5 color families. Once you have cut and sorted them according to the list below, place them in orderly piles, so you can easily see where you are. Cut:

- 16 strips, 17½ in/44 cm long (color A1)

- 32 strips, 16 in/40.5 cm long; 16 in color A2 and 16 in color A3

- 32 strips, 12½ in/32 cm long; 16 in color A4 and 16 in color A5

- 32 strips, 9 in/23 cm long, using leftover scraps (colors A6 and A7)

- 32 strips, 5 in/12 cm long, using leftover scraps (colors A8 and A9)

2. Using the template provided, cut 16 squares, each 12 in/30.5 cm from the craft paper and trace or draw the diagonal lines.

MAKING THE FOUNDATION BLOCKS

(See Foundation Piecing, page 31)

1. Take your prepared paper squares, and starting with the center strip A1, lay this strip, **Right** side up, along the center section, and attach it in place on the paper at the seam allowance with a dab of appliqué glue. Place the next strip (A2), **Right** side down, on one side of the central strip, aligning the raw edges carefully. Using a scant ¼-in/6-mm seam allowance, sew the strips to the paper. Press open. Sew the next strip (A3) in the same way and repeat for the rest of the strips. This can be done production style, sewing all 16 blocks at the same time.

2. When all the strips have been used, press the blocks flat. Using the quilting ruler, cutting mat, and rotary cutter, trim the blocks even with the edges of the paper, then tear away the paper carefully.

COMPLETING THE QUILT TOP

1. Lay the blocks out on a clean surface or design wall, as per the layout diagram. Pin the blocks together at intervals to ensure they line up correctly. Sew them together first

in pairs then in foursomes (2-×-2 grid). Sew the foursomes together, making a 4-×-4 grid, 16-block central panel. Press all seams to one side as you go.

2. Lay out your completed central panel and measure the sides. Cut all the strips for the border along the lengthwise grain of the fabric. From your black fabric, cut one strip 12 in/30.5 cm wide and approximately 93 in/236 cm long. Cut this strip in half, so you end up with two 12-×-46½ in/30.5-×-118-cm strips. Pin these strips to the sides of your quilt and sew in place. Press seams toward the outside edges. Measure the other sides, including the black border, and cut 2 strips from your black border fabric 12 in/30.5 cm wide and approximately 69½ in/77 cm long. Pin these onto the other sides of the central panel and sew in place, completing your border and quilt top.

QUILTING AND FINISHING

For instructions on making the batting and backing, see pages 34 and 36.

1. Layer the quilt top with batting and backing, and baste, using your preferred basting method (see page 37).

2. Using a neutral-color thread (I used mauve, which stands out on the black, but blends into the colored fabrics), machine quilt with an all-over stipple design (see page 40).

3. Following the instructions on page 43, make 300 in/762 cm of continuous straight-cut binding; cut strips 2½ in/6 cm wide. Press and attach the binding in your preferred method (see page 44).

LOLLYPOP TREE

I love the idea of a lollypop tree, and my kids were practically drooling just at the thought of one. The vibrant appliqué lollypop tree in the central panel is surrounded by more subdued tonal floral fabrics in a variation of a Log Cabin block. This "sweet" design is a lot of fun to make and your kids will want to help, as mine did!

Finished quilt size: 64½ in/164 cm square

DIFFICULTY LEVEL **  This quilt is made using a repeat block for the border, and the central panel is made from simple fused machine-sewn appliqué.

FABRIC: 1 Jelly Roll pack of pretty floral fabrics (I used a mix of florals from Lucien). Alternatively, you could get a whole bunch of largish scraps and cut them into 2½-in/ 6-cm strips.

32½-in/83-cm square of white or off-white linen or cotton to use as the background of the central panel

1 pack of solid-color Charm Squares (5 in/12 cm)—or this is a perfect opportunity to make use of your solid-color scrap fabric

BACKING: 3⅞ yds/3.5 m of 44-in-/112-cm-wide cream or unbleached quilting muslin (I used up leftover Jelly Roll strips to add a scrappy strip in an otherwise plain fabric backing)

BATTING: 70-in-/168-cm-square piece of cotton batting

BINDING: ½ yd/46 cm of cotton fabric; use your leftover Jelly Roll strips mixed in with cream fabric for a scrappy binding or use the same fabric as your backing

THREAD: Neutral-color cotton thread suitable for piecing and machine quilting, plus various colored threads to match your appliqué motifs

OTHER INGREDIENTS: Rotary cutter • mat • ruler • scissors • compass • pencil • paper • fusible webbing (1–2 yd/0.9–1.8 m depending on width) • iron

TEMPLATES: Large, medium, and small leaves

NOTES
- Use ¼-in/6-mm seam allowances throughout.
- You will make 12 off-center Log Cabin blocks; trim pieced block to measure 16½ in/ 42 cm square; finished block size is 16 in/40 cm.

PREPARING YOUR FABRIC

1. The Lollypop Tree appliqué designs make use of 3 sizes of circles. You can create your own templates for these using a compass, ruler, pencil, and paper. The dimensions you need are: 4½-in/11.5-cm diameter (large), 2-in/5-cm diameter (medium), and 1-in/2.5-cm diameter (small). Using the templates provided and the ones you created, trace onto the fusible webbing 3 large circles, 12 medium circles, 6 small circles, 4 large leaves, 4 medium leaves, and 4 small leaves.

2. Sew 4 green Charm Squares together to make a 9-in-/ 23-cm-square piece of fabric. Press the seams open, then use the technique described on page 43 to make a continuous single-fold binding strip. You'll use this to form the stem and branches of the lollypop tree. Cut the strip into 5 pieces: one 17-in/43-cm strip, two 6-in/15-cm strips, and two 4-in/10-cm strips.

3. For each block (12 blocks total), cut 2½-in-/6-cm-wide strips as follows:

- 2 strips, 2½ in/6 cm long
- 2 strips, 4½ in/11.5 cm long
- 2 strips, 6¼ in/16 cm long
- 2 strips, 8¼ in/21 cm long
- 2 strips, 10¼ in/26 cm long
- 2 strips, 12 in/30.5 cm long
- 2 strips, 14 in/35.5 cm long
- 1 strip, 16 in/40 cm long

MAKING THE CENTRAL PANEL

1. Prepare your appliqué pieces by cutting roughly around the appliqué motifs that you traced earlier onto the fusible webbing. Place these, sticky side down, onto the **Wrong** side of your scraps of solid-color fabric and press them to fuse. Using small, sharp scissors, cut neatly around the drawn line. Do this for all your appliqué motifs.

2. Cut a strip of fusible webbing to fit the width of your bias binding strips, place the sticky side onto the **Wrong** side of the bias tape, and press with your hot iron to fuse into place.

3. Remove the paper from your bias strips and appliqué motifs and arrange them as desired on the **Right** side of the central panel fabric, using the layout diagram as a guide; be sure to leave at least 1 in/2.5 cm of fabric on all sides of the central panel edges. Use your hot iron to press all the motifs into place.

4. Take this central panel to your sewing machine, match the top thread to the color of each motif when sewing, and sew around the edges of all the appliqué motifs using a zigzag or a blanket stitch. Press this entire piece; the central panel is complete.

MAKING THE BLOCKS

1. Once you have cut all the strips to length according to the cutting instructions, place the same size pieces in separate piles.

2. When sewing, feel free to take them at random or, as I have done, use some of the darker florals to make up the corners of the blocks (this is optional).

3. Follow the block diagram for the sewing order.

4. Press each block to one side as you go.

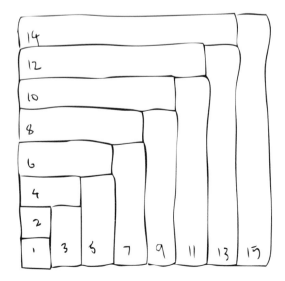

5. To make it easier, try chain piecing the strips; this will allow you to work on all 12 blocks at once, which makes pressing in between more time efficient.

6. Once you've completed all 12 blocks, press them. They should be the same size (16 in/40 cm square); checking that your seam allowance is set to ¼ in/6 mm will help to ensure this. If they are not all the same size, you will need to trim them.

COMPLETING THE QUILT TOP

1. Lay your border blocks around your central panel in a pleasing arrangement. Take the 2 bottom and 2 top blocks and sew them together at the sides; press, then attach these to your central panel.

2. Take the 4 blocks on either side and sew these into a strip; press the seams and then attach to the sides of the central panel. Press the entire quilt top.

QUILTING AND FINISHING

For instructions on making the batting and backing, see pages 34 and 36.

1. Layer the quilt top with batting and backing, and baste, using your preferred basting method (see page 37).

2. Using a thread that matches your central panel background, machine quilt with an all-over, medium-size stipple design (see page 40). Be sure to quilt up to and around the lollypop tree design.

3. Following the instructions on page 43 to make 270 in/ 686 cm of continuous straight-cut binding; cut strips 2½ in/ 6 cm wide. Press and attach the binding in your preferred method (see page 44).

LAYER CAKES

Layer Cakes, also an invention of Moda Fabrics, are pre-cut 10-in/25-cm squares. They come in a pack of 40 and contain all the prints within a collection and some duplicates as well. They are a perfect way to get a good taste of a bunch of fabric in one hit. Layer Cakes are versatile—sewing them together as they are makes for a quick and easy quilt, or you can cut them into a whole heap of different variations. Cutting them into quarters results in four 5-in/12-cm squares; or if you cut them into 8 triangles, you can make a flying geese block.

For 3 of the quilts in this section, I made my own collection of 10-in/25-cm Layer Cakes from fabrics in my stash using a 10-in/25-cm square ruler, cutting mat, and rotary cutter. I wanted a look that I couldn't get from any of the collections I saw. I used Paula Prass's Summer Soiree collection by Michael Miller, some delightful '30s reproduction fabrics and a lot of checks, stripes, and plaids that just begged to be used together. Cutting Layer Cakes yourself means you can use up some of the larger scraps from your collection. You might even want to spend a day trimming some of your leftovers and making a few Layer Cakes sets— tie them up with a ribbon or store them in zip-lock bags for a future project. For the other two quilts, I used Moda collections, Rouenneries by French General, and Botany by Lauren + Jessi Jung.

The following projects are included in this chapter,
all using Layer Cakes:

DRESS CIRCLE: **   **PRISMATIC: **

CRIMSON CROSS: *   **SUNNY DAY MAT: ****

POP WREATH: **

DRESS CIRCLE

My blind desire to make a circle quilt, plus seeing how well the 1930s reproduction prints teamed with the delicious Kona Solids Charm Squares, inspired this quilt design. My nerdy hubby also likes the way the background square is echoed in the hexagon, which also creates a 3D cube if you half close your eyes. This design is suitable for all ages and I find it especially lovely as a snuggly couch throw.

<u>**Finished quilt size:**</u> 63½ in/161 cm square

DIFFICULTY LEVEL **✱✱**

Raw edge appliqué with fusible webbing, simple sewing of squares, and an offset vertical layout are used in this simple quilt.

FABRIC: Just under 1 pack of Layer Cakes; or 37 squares (10 in/25 cm)

4 packs of bright solid-color 5-in/12-cm Charm Squares; or 100 squares (5 in/12 cm) cut from 8 Fat Quarters

BACKGROUND: 2 yd/1.8 m of 44-in-/112-cm-wide off-white quilting cotton fabric

BACKING: 4 yd/3.7 m of 44-in-/112-cm-wide cotton fabric of your choice (I used a simple off-white muslin backing)

BATTING: 70-in-/178-cm-square piece of cotton batting

BINDING: ½ yd/46 cm of 44-in-/112-cm-wide fabric to match your background fabric or complement your colors. A striped or a scrappy solid binding would be perfect.

DOUBLE SIDED FUSIBLE WEBBING: approximately 2 yd/1.8 m, depending on width of roll

THREAD: Natural- or cream-color cotton thread suitable for piecing and quilting, plus various colored machine threads to match your fabric circles

OTHER INGREDIENTS: compass • 10-in/25-cm ruler • pencil • scissors • rotary cutter • mat • paper • 5-in-/12-cm-wide quilting ruler

---

NOTES

• Use ¼-in/6-mm seam allowances throughout.

• Full block finished size is 9 in/23 cm square.

PREPARING YOUR FABRIC

1. To make your circle template for the circle appliqué shapes, use a compass, ruler, and pencil to draw a circle, 7 in/17.5 cm in diameter. Cut out your template and use it to trace 37 circles onto the double-sided fusible webbing. Roughly cut around them and fuse them to the **Wrong** side of your Layer Cakes squares. Neatly cut around the circles (there will be some leftover fabric from each 10-in/25-cm square—save this for a scrappy quilt.

2. Cut 18 plain 9½-in/24-cm squares from your background fabric, using the 10-in/25-cm ruler. Cut 12 plain 9½-×-5-in/ 24-×-12-cm pieces from your background fabric, using the 5-in-/12-cm-wide ruler.

MAKING THE QUILT TOP

1. Sew 23 Charm Square 4-×-4 grid blocks; use the chain piecing method (see page 32) for quick piecing—first sewing in pairs, then in foursomes.

2. Sew 4 blocks with one pair of Charm Squares and one half size (9½-×-5-in/24-×-12 cm) background block.

3. Fuse 10 of the circles onto 10 of the 9½-in-/24-cm-square plain blocks.

4. Fuse 4 of the circles onto the half plain, half Charm Square blocks.

5. Fuse 23 of the circles onto the 23 Charm Square 4-×-4 blocks.

6. Once you have fused the circle appliqués onto their respective blocks, take them all to the sewing machine. Using a thread that matches the circle motif (not the background fabric), machine sew around the outside edge of each circle motif with a zigzag or blanket stitch.

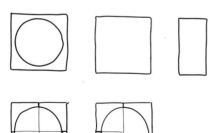

7. Lay the completed blocks and the remaining plain square and half-square blocks out onto your clean floor, or your design wall, and arrange as per the layout diagram. Check the placement of color so you don't have too many of the same colors near each other. Sew them together in vertical rows and press the seams in each row in an alternating direction. Then pin the rows together, at intervals to match seams, and sew. Press the seams to one side as you go. Your quilt top is now complete.

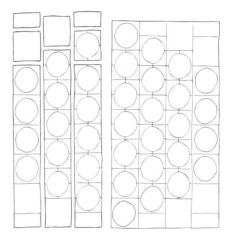

QUILTING AND FINISHING

For instructions on making the batting and backing, see pages 34 and 36.

1. Layer the quilt top with batting and backing, and baste, using your preferred basting method (see page 37).

2. Using a neutral- or cream-color thread, machine quilt over the entire surface with an all-over fill design (see page 40). I used a medium-dense scribble design; a stipple would be equally good, or use your own preferred design.

3. Follow the instructions on page 43 make 280 in/711 cm of continuous straight-cut binding; cut strips 2½ in/6 cm wide. Press and attach the binding in your preferred method (see page 44).

PRISMATIC

I think of this quilt as super-modern. The use of bright white as a background, teamed with an eclectic but cohesive combination of print fabrics in aqua, lime green, lemon yellow, hot pink, and grey, has created a contemporary design perfect for all ages but especially appealing to younger folks. When I was trying to think of a name for this block, I again asked my husband Rob for help: He replied that it had a "Prismatic sort of feel to it." It stuck!

Finished quilt size: 72½ × 90½ in/184 × 230 cm

DIFFICULTY LEVEL **✳✳**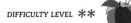

This quilt is really a very simple design. The basic triangle block is very versatile; you'll notice yourself finding more excuses to use it. This block is simple to make, and putting it together is fun and challenging—a great outcome for comparatively little effort.

FABRIC: 1 pack of Layer Cakes (10 in/25 cm) in bright, cheerful colors (I made my own set of layer cakes using fabric from Summer Soiree by Paula Prass for Michael Miller)

3 yd/2.7 m of 44-in-/112-cm-wide white cotton fabric for the front. White makes this quilt super modern; if you want the same design with a different feel, use a creamy white for a softer result, or a dark grey for a more masculine feel.

BACKING: 3 yd/2.7 m of 44-in-/112-cm-wide coordinating cotton fabric

BATTING: 80-×-95 in/203-×-241-cm piece of cotton batting

BINDING: ¾ yd/70 cm of 44-in-/112-cm-wide white cotton fabric or use the same fabric you used for the triangles in the quilt top

THREAD: White cotton thread suitable for piecing and machine quilting

OTHER INGREDIENTS: Rotary cutter • mat • 10-in/25-cm square ruler • pencil • pins

---
NOTES
- Use ¼-in/6-mm seam allowances throughout.
- Accurate seam allowances will ensure perfect points that meet up every time.
- Finished block size is 9 in/23 cm square.

PREPARING YOUR FABRIC

1. If you're not using Layer Cakes, cut 40 squares (10 in/25 cm) from your patterned fabric.

2. Cut 40 squares (10 in/25 cm) from the white fabric.

MAKING UP THE BLOCKS

1. Place a white square on top of a print square lining them up perfectly, and pin together. Using a pencil and ruler, draw a line from one corner to the other. Do this for all of the blocks. Now take them to your sewing machine and using the chain-piecing method (see page 32), sew a ¼-in/6-mm seam on either side of the drawn line.

2. Using the rotary cutter, ruler, and mat, cut the squares apart, directly on the drawn line, one at a time. Open them out to reveal a triangle block 9½ in/24 cm square. Press the seams to one side. You will have 80 of these blocks. (This method is described on page 33.)

COMPLETING THE QUILT TOP

1. Lay out your blocks on a clean surface, using the layout diagram as a guide. Mix up the blocks so you have a good range of color and fabric. This is the trickiest part of the whole design—ensuring the white triangles are in the correct orientation so you don't mess up the design.

2. Pin each square to the next one while they are on the floor and then take a chain of pinned pieces to the sewing machine. This way you won't lose track of their placement while sewing. Sew the squares in rows. Make sure to keep to a ¼-in/6-mm seam allowance to allow you to match up your corners when sewing the rows together. Press the seams of each row in an alternate direction.

3. Pin each row at the seams to ensure that they match up perfectly and sew the rows together. Press the top.

QUILTING AND FINISHING

For instructions on making the batting and backing, see pages 34 and 36.

1. Layer the quilt top with batting and backing, and baste, using your preferred basting method (see page 37).

2. Using white thread, machine quilt with an all-over design (see page 40). I used a somewhat geometric echo quilting design, just for something different.

3. Following the instructions on page 43, make 345 in/ 876 cm of continuous straight-cut binding; cut strips 2½ in/ 6 cm wide. Press and attach the binding in your preferred method (see page 44).

CRIMSON CROSS

This cross quilt is my version of the classic Red Cross quilt, which was often made by charity groups as a fundraising effort. I have always admired the design of the Red Cross quilt. I've adapted and simplified it in order to use pre-cut strips. This block design is also the basis of the Across the Globe Friendship Quilt on page 13. It makes a perfect design for charity, quilting bees, or block swaps.

Finished quilt size: 80½ × 90 ½ in/204 × 230 cm

DIFFICULTY LEVEL **✳**

This quilt is very simple to make. The blocks are a pleasure to construct, using a "recipe" rather than a strict pattern; the only tricky bit comes with putting them together in the quilt top. As it is quite a big quilt, manipulating the quilt top under the sewing machine as it grows can be a little unwieldy.

FABRIC: 2 packs of Layer Cakes (I used Rouenneries by French General for Moda)

1 pack of Honey Buns. These are 1½-in-/4-cm-wide pre-cut strips; like Jelly Rolls, these are cut selvage to selvage.

BACKING: 5 yd/4.6 m of 44-in-/112-cm-wide cotton fabric in a complementary color

BATTING: 85-×-95-in/216-×-241-cm piece of cotton batting

BINDING: ¾ yd/70 cm of cotton fabric in a complementary color

THREAD: Neutral-color cotton thread suitable for piecing and machine quilting

OTHER INGREDIENTS: Rotary cutter • mat • ruler

NOTES
- Use ¼-in/6-mm seam allowances throughout.
- Finished block size is 10 in/25 cm square.

PREPARING YOUR FABRIC

1. Place 6 Layer Cakes squares neatly on top of one another on the cutting mat. Using the ruler and rotary cutter, cut down one side, parallel to the edge. Do this to all of the Layer Cakes squares, keeping them with their other halves. Cut some directly in the center, and others off center to varying degrees to give some variety in the quilt block designs.

2. Cut all of the Honey Bun strips in half along the center crease; they will measure 1½ × 22 in/4 × 56 cm after cutting.

3. Sort your squares and strips into pleasing color combinations, making sure you have one strip paired with each of the cut Layer Cakes squares. If you're planning on chain piecing the blocks, be sure to keep yourself organized so that you don't lose track of the other sections of the block as you go.

MAKING THE BLOCKS

1. Take one set of the paired-up strips and Layer Cake squares, and sew the strip to the center of the 2 halves of the square. Trim off the excess length of the strip and keep the rest of the strip with the block. Press the seams toward the outside edges. Repeat this step on the remaining sets of strips and cut squares.

2. Cut the blocks again, at right angles to the first strip. Cut some directly in the center, and others off center to varying degrees. Sew the remaining piece of the strip in the center of the two halves. Press seams toward the outside edges and your basic block is complete.

COMPLETING THE QUILT TOP

1. Lay your blocks out on a large flat surface, arranging them in a pleasing design, 8 blocks wide by 9 blocks high, so that no two like blocks are next to each other. If you like, you can arrange the blocks so that there is a subtle color/tone gradient as I did.

2. Pin each square to the next while they are on the floor and then take a chain of pinned pieces to the sewing machine. This way, you won't lose track of their placement while sewing. Sew the blocks together in rows. Be sure to keep to a ¼-in/6-mm seam allowance to allow you to match up your corners when sewing the rows together. Press the seams in each different row in an alternate direction.

3. Pin each row at the seams to ensure the seams match up perfectly and sew the rows together. Press the top.

QUILTING AND FINISHING

For instructions on making the batting and backing, see pages 34 and 36.

1. Layer the quilt top with batting and backing, and baste, using your preferred basting method (see page 37).

2. Using a neutral-color thread, machine quilt with an all-over stipple design (see page 40).

3. Following the instructions on page 43 make 350 in/890 cm of continuous straight-cut binding; cut strips 2½ in/6 cm wide. Press and attach the binding in your preferred method (see page 44).

4. With the leftover Layer Cakes pieces, you might like to make some matching cushions to place on your bed.

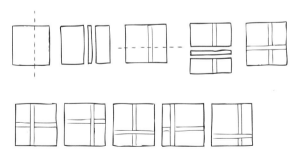

SUNNY DAY MAT

This play mat with its textured center and prairie point edging gives baby something interesting to play on. However, the appeal of this mat goes further than babies—my mother wants it for her coffee table and my daughter wants it for her reading space. I might have to whip up a couple more of these!

Finished quilt size: 48-in-/122-cm-diameter circle

DIFFICULTY LEVEL ✳✳✳✳ This quilt has some tricky triangles to piece to make the star design and sewing the circular sections together requires careful pinning. Plus there are the prairie points to add around the edge. However, because it's small, it can still likely be a weekend project.

FABRIC: 1 pack of Layer Cakes (I used Botany by Lauren+Jessi Jung for Moda). Choose 7 different pieces from the pack to use for the wedges. Most of the remaining Layer Cakes pieces will be used to make your prairie points and there will be a few left over for a future project.

7 Fat Quarters in solid sunny colors (I used yellows and greens from Amy Butler's and Moda's solids collections)

14-in-/36-cm-square piece of chenille or other textured fabric in a coordinating color

BACKING: 1⅜ yd/1.3 m of a 44-in-/112-cm-wide multicolored dark fabric (so that the dirt doesn't show, if it's to be used as a floor mat)

BATTING: 55-in-/140-cm-square piece of cotton batting for a sturdy machine washable floor mat

BINDING: ½ yd/46 cm of the same fabric as your backing

THREAD: Neutral-color cotton thread suitable for piecing and machine quilting

OTHER INGREDIENTS: Rotary cutter • mat • quilting ruler • iron • pen/pencil • compass • card stock or plastic to make template pieces • pins

TEMPLATES: Small triangle, large triangle, and wedge piece

> **NOTE**
> • Use ¼-in/6-mm seam allowances throughout.

PREPARING YOUR FABRIC

1. Trace the template pieces onto card stock or plastic—there are 2 triangle shapes and 1 wedge shape. To make the center circle, use a compass, ruler, and pencil to draw a 13-in-/33-cm-diameter circle onto card stock, and cut the circle out. Check this template against your completed inner ring before cutting it out in fabric, adjusting as needed.

2. Cut 32 wedge shapes from the 7 different Layer Cakes pieces.

3. Cut the remaining Layer Cakes squares into quarters and make approximately 60 folded prairie points using the instructions on page 45.

4. Use 2 Fat Quarters to cut 16 of the small triangle shape.

5. Use 5 Fat Quarters to cut 16 of the large triangle shape.

6. Cut the center circle from the chenille fabric.

MAKING THE QUILT TOP

1. Sew the wedges, long sides together, in one long strip to form a giant ring. Press the seams to one side when you have finished sewing them all.

2. Following the layout diagram, sew the triangles together to form the outer ring. Sew these one at a time, pressing in between and ensuring each time that you have a ¼-in/6-mm seam allowance on the point so that you don't lose the points when you sew the rings together. This is the tricky bit, and the only way to get it correct is to be sure your cutting, pinning, and seam allowances are all accurate.

3. Once you have your inner and outer rings completed, lay the inner ring of wedge pieces on a flat surface and place the outer ring around it, matching up the base of the star points with the seam between two of the wedges. Place the rings **Right** sides together and pin the matched points at intervals all the way around. Sew together, then press the seam to the side where it naturally falls.

4. Lay out what you've constructed so far, and place the chenille center circle over the top of the inner ring, **Right** side up; pin it in place. Top stitch around with a zigzag stitch and leave the seam edge raw. Press the entire quilt top.

QUILTING AND FINISHING

For instructions on making the batting and backing, see pages 34 and 36.

1. Layer the quilt top with batting and backing, and baste, using your preferred basting method (see page 37).

2. Using a neutral-color thread, machine quilt with an all-over squiggle design (see page 40).

3. Following the instructions on page 43, make 330 in/838 cm of continuous bias-cut binding; cut strips 2½ in/6 cm wide.

4. Lay out your prairie points all around the quilt, **Right** sides down, with the raw edges of the prairie points lining up with the raw edges of the quilt, and with each prairie point tucked into the fold of the one in front of it. If you want to use more points, you can arrange them closer together; if you want a few left over for another project, they can be arranged with a little more breathing space. Pin these and sew a ⅛-in/3-mm basting stitch around them to hold them in place.

5. Place the raw edges of your binding strips along the raw edges of the quilt, sandwiching the prairie points between them. Machine stitch the binding to the quilt top with a ¼-in/6-mm seam allowance and then hand stitch to the back. Follow the instructions for facing a quilt on page 46. Your mat is now finished—enjoy!

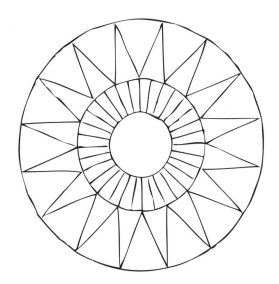

POP WREATH

A classic wreath-style quilt, usually consisting of ornate intertwining vines, is simplified here by the use of large concentric circles. The fabric is a combination of checks, plaids, stripes, and polka dots, which gives the quilt a very modern yet soft appearance. Hand quilting extends the softness and enhances the modest appeal of this quilt.

Finished quilt size: 79 in/201 cm square—perfect for a double bed
(this measurement doesn't include the scallop trim)

DIFFICULTY LEVEL ✳✳✳✳

This is a fairly simple design; however, the fact that the appliqué is hand sewn using the needle turn method, and has also been hand quilted, makes it a bit of a long-term project. You can speed it up by machine sewing the appliqué and machine quilting, which will give the quilt a completely different look.

FABRIC: 2 packs of pre-cut Layer Cakes squares (10 in/25 cm), 40 squares in each pack, in a modern pretty fabric (I chose a combination of polka dots, stripes, plaids, and checks)

BACKGROUND: 4½ yd/4.1 m of 44-in-/112-cm-wide white or off-white plain cotton fabric

BACKING: 5½ yd/5 m of 44-in-/112-cm-wide polka dot or white fabric for the backing and the back of the scallops

BATTING: 85-in-/216-cm-square piece of wool batting or thin cotton batting if you are hand quilting, or regular cotton batting if you are machine quilting

BINDING: ¾ yd/70 cm of fabric to match backing fabric

THREAD: Neutral-color thread suitable for machine and hand sewing, plus white coated hand-quilting thread for hand quilting

OTHER INGREDIENTS: Card stock or paper for tracing • pencil • scissors • appliqué needles • water-soluble fabric marking pencil • hand-quilting needles • appliqué glue • thimble • quilting or embroidery hoop • beeswax if you are not using coated hand-quilting thread

TEMPLATES: Circle shapes, leaf shape (in template envelope)

NOTES

- Use ¼-in/6-mm seam allowances for all sewing except where indicated for the appliqué motifs.
- Finished block size is 39½ in/102 cm square.

PREPARING YOUR FABRIC

1. Sort your Layer Cakes fabrics into colors suitable for the leaves and stems. (I saved all the greens.)

2. Trace the templates onto card stock or paper to create the patterns. A ½-in/12-mm seam allowance has been included on the template pieces.

3. Trace and cut your templates:

- 16 medium circles and 16 small circles from 16 of the 10-in/25-cm squares

- 16 large circles from 16 of the 10-in/25-cm squares

- 4 leaves per 10-in/25-cm square from 12 of the squares, for a total of 48 leaves

- Four 40-in/102-cm squares from your background fabric

4. Cut 24 scallop shapes from 24 of the 10-in/25-cm squares. (No template is provided.) Round off the 2 top corners, using a dinner plate to make the scallop shape. Cut another 24 scallop shapes from 1 yd/91 cm of backing fabric.

5. From the remaining 9 green 10-in/25-cm squares, make your bias binding for the circular bias vines. Sew these Layer Cakes squares into a 3-×-3 block, then follow the instructions on page 43 to make continuous bias binding, cutting it into 2½-in-/6-cm-wide strips. Fold, then use your iron to press the long raw edges in toward the center (see page 43).

6. Make a circle template from card stock for each of the circle shapes, minus the ½-in/12-mm seam allowance. Run a basting stitch around the outside edge of the fabric circles within the seam allowance (you don't want this stitch line to be seen later). Place a template inside a fabric circle, pull the stitches to gather them around the template, and press the seam over the template edge. Remove the template. Do this for all of your circles.

7. Make the leaf shapes in the same way as the circles; however, for the tips of the leaves, fold the fabric to a point rather than gathering them in.

MAKING THE QUILT TOP

1. Lay your motif elements on each of the 40-in/102-cm squares of background fabric, as per the layout diagram, layering the circles in groups of three, and pin. Place and pin the bias vines into position, pressing gently as you go to create the curves. Place the ends of the vines underneath the circles. Place the tips of the leaves just underneath the vines; pin, then tack or use a little appliqué glue to hold the pieces in position.

2. Use a quilting or embroidery hoop to hold the fabric in position. Using a coordinating thread, hand sew around the edge of each motif with a blind stitch (see page 48). Repeat for the other 3 blocks in the same way. Sew the four blocks together to complete your quilt top.

MAKING SCALLOPS FOR THE EDGING

1. Place 1 Layer Cake scallop piece and 1 backing fabric scallop piece **Right** sides together, aligning the edges.

2. Sew around the curved edge, leaving the straight edges open; chain piecing (see page 32) makes this a breeze.

3. Turn each scallop **Right** side out and press flat. Put these aside for use later.

QUILTING AND FINISHING

For instructions on making the batting and backing, see pages 34 and 36.

1. Layer the quilt top with batting and backing, and baste, using a large tacking stitch (see page 37).

2. Using a water-soluble fabric marking pencil, mark your quilt top in the design you wish to quilt. Here, an echo quilting design 1 in/2.5 cm apart was used, with a more decorative quilting design in the center of each circle.

3. Use a quilting or embroidery hoop to hold the quilt layers taut while you quilt and a waxed hand-quilting thread to match your background fabric. You'll also need special quilting needles and a thimble. See the instructions on page 38 for how to hand quilt.

4. Follow the instructions on page 43 to make 330 in/838 cm of continuous straight-cut binding; cut strips 2½ in/6 cm wide.

5. Lay out your quilt, face up, somewhere clean. Place your scallop shapes around the edges, **Right** sides down, with the scallop raw edges lining up with the raw edges of the quilt top. Place the scallops along the two sides and the bottom of your quilt—leave the top edge, where you sleep, free of scallops so that they do not tickle your chin. Once you're sure the scallops are evenly spaced, tack or pin them into place.

6. Place the raw edges of the binding along the raw edges of the quilt, sandwiching the scallop shapes between them. Machine sew the binding to the quilt top, and hand sew it to the back. Follow the instructions for facing a quilt on page 46.

7. Your quilt is now ready to be used. As it is primarily hand stitched and hand quilted, I would recommend hand washing and line drying only. This is perfect as a bedroom quilt for special occasions.

FAT QUARTERS

Fat Quarters are typically a quarter of a yard, approximately 18 x 22 in/ 46 x 56 cm, but may vary slightly depending on the width of the fabric. A Fat Quarter of fabric is much more useful than a skinny quarter yard (9 x 44 in/ 23 x 112 cm); its versatility for both patchwork and appliqué (and in stash building) makes it one of the most popular pre-cuts available. Patchwork shops will have a variety of Fat Quarters ready-cut from their popular ranges, ready for you to buy on a whim; they are great for swaps.

Fat Quarters in Australia, New Zealand, and Europe, where the metric measurement system is used, are cut as a quarter meter of fabric and are slightly bigger than a quarter yard (20 x 22 in/50 x 56 cm). However, you may find some pre-cut Fat Quarters billed as American Fat Quarters—if in doubt, ask.

For the five quilts in this section, I've used a variety of fabrics; these or ones very similar are available in most fabric stores and online. For Floral Notes I used batik marbled hand-dyed fabrics from Island Batiks; Anna Maria Horner's Good Folks collection is a richly colored fabric range that works like a kaleidoscope in Garnets and Gold; and I used soft chalky colors by Amy Butler from Westminster Fabrics in Sewing Circle. 5 Flavors uses five different solid-colored fabrics from Moda Fabrics, and Summer Sundae uses Sweet by Urban Chiks for Moda.

The following projects are included in this chapter, all using Fat Quarters:

GARNETS AND GOLD: ****   **5 FLAVORS:** ****

FLORAL NOTES: ***   **SUMMER SUNDAE:** ****

SEWING CIRCLE: ****

GARNETS AND GOLD

Do you remember those kaleidoscope toys you had as a kid? Do you remember being amazed by the constantly changing pattern of shapes and dazzling colors? This quilt is my homage to visual illusions—a basic block made of triangle shapes that clash to tease and confuse the eye. With the help of a jewel-like fabric, the quilt becomes a rich tapestry of possibility.

Finished quilt size: 60 × 85½ in/152 × 217 cm

DIFFICULTY LEVEL ✳✳✳✳

The accuracy required when cutting and piecing makes this quilt rather tricky. It is important to match up the large diamond shapes formed by the blue and green triangles, and not so important to worry where 12 points all come together. It is difficult to get them all perfect. The 12 points will likely come together in a jagged corner, but that just adds to the fun kaleidoscope effect of this quilt.

FABRIC: 12 Fat Quarters (18 × 22 in/46 × 56 cm) in rich jewel colors—lapis lazuli, jade, emerald, and sapphire (i.e., blues, aquas, and greens)

14 Fat Quarters in golden tones—garnet, ruby, and amethyst (i.e., yellows, pinks, and magenta)

BACKING: 4 yd/3.7 m of 44-in-/112-cm-wide coordinating fabric (I used 2 pieces, 2 yd/1.8 m each, and connected them with some scraps)

BATTING: 65-×-90-in-/165-×-229-cm piece of cotton batting

BINDING: ⅝ yd/76 cm of 44-in-/112-cm-wide cotton fabric in a coordinating color

THREAD: Neutral-color cotton thread for piecing and dark-color cotton thread that blends in with your color fabrics for quilting

OTHER INGREDIENTS: Rotary cutter • mat • ruler • freezer paper • pencil

TEMPLATES: Left-side + right-side A triangle and left-side + right-side B triangle

NOTES

- Use ¼-in/6-mm seam allowances throughout.
- Finished block size is 8½ in/21.5 cm square; make 70 (35 left and 35 right) blocks.
- Because the edges of the triangle pieces are on the bias, you must be careful not to pull at them; doing this will stretch them out of shape.
- Accurate cutting is important to get the most out of each Fat Quarter; you should get 14–16 A triangles from a Fat Quarter and 10–12 B triangles from a Fat Quarter. When cutting, place the top edge of the triangles on the straight grain to minimize stretching of the pieces; this might mean a little more fabric wastage.

Quilt top sewn by Chris Hayes

PREPARING THE FABRIC

1. Using the templates provided, trace the four triangle shapes onto the freezer paper. Cut out the pieces and label them.

2. Cut 70 left-side A triangles and 70 right-side A triangles in rich blue and green jewel tones.

3. Cut 70 left-side B triangles and 70 right-side B triangles in pink, magenta, and golden tones.

4. Lay your pieces out before sewing them together—a design wall is perfect for this, but a clean floor is a good second best. Separate out the left-side and right-side blocks and arrange them in piles.

MAKING THE BASIC BLOCKS

1. When sewing the pieces together, you can chain piece (see page 32) them to speed up the process. Begin with two center triangles (B), then attach the outside right-angle triangles to form the basic block (see layout diagram). Make 35 right-side blocks and 35 left-side blocks. Press the seams on the left blocks to the left and the seams on the right blocks to the right.

 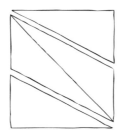

2. Lay out your blocks again, using the diagram as a guide and ensuring a good mix of color throughout. Take 2 right-side and 2 left-side blocks and arrange them as per the diagram. Sew together in sets of four, matching up your points as best you can. Prioritize the point where the blue/green right-angle triangles meet up to make the large blue/green central diamonds—getting this right is important. Press the seams so that they all go clockwise.

COMPLETING THE QUILT TOP

Follow the layout diagram when sewing the foursomes together; sew them into sections of eight, then sew these together to finish your quilt. Press as you go, then press the entire quilt top flat.

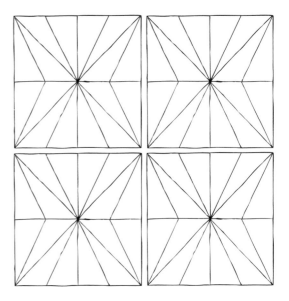

QUILTING AND FINISHING

For instructions on making the batting and backing, see pages 34 and 36.

1. Layer the quilt top with batting and backing, and baste, using your preferred basting method (see page 37).

2. Using a dark-color thread (a dark color such as grey or mauve is perfect to blend in with the colorful fabrics), machine quilt with a large echo-style stipple design (see page 40).

3. Following the instructions on page 43, make 320 in/ 813 cm of continuous straight-cut binding; cut strips 2½ in/ 6 cm wide. Press and attach the binding in your preferred method (see page 44).

5 FLAVORS

This quilt is named for and inspired by colorful candy. It uses five fruity flavors—blueberry, mint, orange, raspberry, and lemon—but you might want to choose your own favorite flavors. How about the classic line-up of lemon, lime, orange, cherry, and pineapple? An island fruits combo in chalky pastels would be cool also. This quilt uses foundation pieced and appliquéd blocks alternating in a grid pattern; be sure to mix the colors around so no two colors are near each other.

Finished quilt size: 52 × 65 in/132 × 165 cm

DIFFICULTY LEVEL **★★★★** The foundation pieced blocks alternate with appliqué blocks and are quilted with a tight pebble design; this means that the quilt is going to take a bit of time. However, if you make the blocks production-line style, you'll save time.

FABRIC: 10 Fat Quarters (18 × 22 in/46 × 56 cm) in 5 flavors of solid-color fabric (2 Fat Quarters, or ½ yd/46 cm each color)

BACKGROUND: 1½ yd/1.4 m of 44-in-/112-cm-wide cream-color cotton fabric for the base of the appliqué blocks

BACKING: 3 yd/2.7 m of 44-in-/112-cm-wide cotton fabric in a coordinating color (I used a bright yellow stripe)

BATTING: 57-×-70-in/140-×-178-cm piece of cotton batting

BINDING: ½ yd/46 cm of fabric in the same color as your backing—this binding will be used to face the quilt and will not be seen from the front

THREAD: Neutral-color cotton thread suitable for piecing and machine quilting, and various colors to match your 5 flavors of fabric appliqué

OTHER INGREDIENTS: Rotary cutter • mat • quilting ruler • pencil • freezer paper • compass • card stock • craft paper for foundation piecing • appliqué glue (or pins) • scissors • iron

TEMPLATES: Foundation pattern for block #1

NOTES

- Use ¼-in/6-mm seam allowances throughout, except your circle motif where you will use ½-in/12-mm seam allowances.
- Pieced block measures 13½ in/34 cm square; finished block size is 13 in/33 cm square.
- Two different block styles are used for this quilt: foundation pieced diagonal blocks and ring-shaped appliqué blocks. Make 10 of each.

continued

- Do not use fusible webbing on your appliqué; instead use appliqué glue to hold them in position while you sew. After you wash the quilt, the appliqué rings will puff out slightly.

- Faced binding is used on this quilt, so that no binding is showing at the front. If you're not ready for this method and you want to use regular binding, match your binding to the cream-color background fabric.

- When making your foundation blocks, carefully measure out the fabric so there is no waste; this means that you need to be very careful when lining up your strips to sew.

PREPARING YOUR FABRIC

1. Cut 10 squares (13½ in/34 cm) from your background fabric; these will form the base for your appliqué blocks.

2. Cut 5 Fat Quarters (one of each color) into 4-×-22-in/ 10-×-56-cm strips.

3. Cut another 2 strips (4 × 22 in/10 × 56 cm) from the remaining 5 Fat Quarters for a total of 6 strips (4 × 22 in/ 10 × 56 cm) of each color.

4. To make the template for the ring appliqué, use a compass, pencil, and ruler to draw a 10-in-/25.5-cm-diameter circle onto card stock. Then, use the same center point to draw a 1.5-in-/4-cm-diameter inner circle. This allows a ½-in/ 12-mm seam allowance. Cut out your template. Trace 10 ring motifs onto freezer paper, and cut these out. Iron the freezer paper rings onto the remaining section of each of the 5 Fat Quarters, 2 rings per Fat Quarter. Cut out, leaving a ½-in/12-mm seam allowance around the outside and the inside of the rings.

5. Using the template provided, cut 10 squares (13½ in/ 34 cm) from the craft paper and draw the diagonal lines.

MAKING THE FOUNDATION BLOCKS

1. Use 2 of your prepared paper squares at a time; making these in pairs is a good idea as for each 2 blocks, you will use 2 strips of one color and 4 strips of each of the remaining colors (the leftovers of which will be used in subsequent pairs of blocks). Sort your fabric strips into groups per pair of blocks and place with a foundation square of paper (see page 32 for foundation piecing tips).

2. Begin with 2 strips of the same color, and make these the center strip of each block. Lay this strip, **Right** side up, and attach it in place to the paper square along the seam allowance with a dab of appliqué glue; then choose two other strips to attach to either side of this central strip. Place a strip, **Right** side down on the center strip, aligning it carefully and sew the strips to the paper, using a scant ¼-in/ 6-mm seam allowance. Press the 2 strips open. Sew the other strip onto the other side of the central strip in the same way. Repeat this for the other block using the other 2 colors. Sew your last color strip onto the outside of the blocks in the same way. Be thrifty with your strips as the leftovers of these will be used on the remaining blocks.

3. Your first 2 blocks are completed. The leftover sections of the outer strips will be used in the subsequent blocks. To ensure you get the most from the strips, carefully align the strips so there is absolutely no waste and make sure you don't repeat any of the same colors within the same block.

4. Use the quilting ruler, cutting mat, and rotary cutter to trim the blocks to the edge of the paper. Then carefully rip away the paper for lovely neat seams and perfectly aligned diagonals.

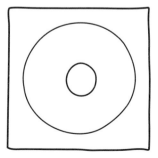 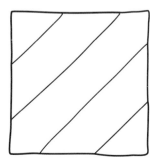

MAKING THE APPLIQUÉ RING BLOCK

1. Take your ring fabric motifs, with the freezer paper still attached, and with your sewing machine set to its longest straight stitch and the tension loosened, sew around the outside of each of the circles, within the seam allowance. Do not backstitch at all. The circles will just naturally curve around the paper. Press around each circle with a hot iron. (See page 47 for more on this method.)

2. To fold under the inner circle seam allowance, neatly clip this inner seam all around, using small, sharp scissors. There is no shortcut for doing this, and this task tends to be a bit fiddly; fold this seam allowance over the freezer paper and press as you go. When the seam allowances have been pressed to the **Wrong** side, remove the freezer paper.

3. Find the center point of the plain fabric squares by folding them into quarters and finger pressing the corner seams. Use this central point to correctly align your ring motifs. Attach your ring motif to the background square using a dab of appliqué glue just under the seam allowance—put a dab every inch or so around to hold it in place while you sew.

4. Using a top thread that matches the color of the appliqué motif, machine sew carefully around the outside and inside circumferences with a small zigzag or blanket stitch. If you would rather that no stitching show, hand sew these with an invisible blind stitch (see page 48).

COMPLETING THE QUILT TOP

1. Lay out your completed squares alternating a circle appliqué block with a diagonal strip block, ensuring a good mix of color variation over the quilt, and ensuring that the diagonal blocks are all facing in the same direction. To ensure that the corners match correctly, pin before sewing, pinning carefully so as not to stretch the diagonal blocks out of shape.

2. Sew together the blocks, first in pairs, then in sets of 4, then the rest to complete your quilt top. Press the seams to one side.

QUILTING AND FINISHING

For instructions on making the batting and backing, see pages 34 and 36.

1. Layer the quilt top with batting and backing, and baste, using your preferred basting method (see page 37).

2. Using a neutral-color thread, machine quilt with an all-over free-motion design (see page 40). I used a pebble stitch, which is a time- and thread-consuming design, but extremely effective and visually appealing. Leave the rings unquilted—just quilt up to and around the edges and in the centers of the rings, allowing the rings to puff out.

3. Following the instructions on page 43, make 250 in/ 635 cm of continuous straight-cut binding; cut strips 2½ in/ 6 cm wide. Press and attach the binding using the faced binding method (see page 46), leaving a clean edge at the front.

4. If you will be using this quilt as a hanging quilt, you will need to attach a hanging sleeve (see page 50). Your quilt is now finished.

FLORAL NOTES

This spring flower quilt is perfect for a pretty, bright room. It will fit a double bed, but can be adapted easily to a smaller size—all you need to do is make less blocks. The flower motifs seem bold and modern, but many of them are actually based on traditional Album Quilts and some have a folk-art feel. The design can be personalized by swapping in some of your own flower motifs.

Finished quilt size: 86½ in/219 cm square

DIFFICULTY LEVEL ✳✳✳   This quilt involves easy appliqué and requires you to cut out a lot of shapes, but as the designs are big, the sewing is surprisingly easy.

FABRIC: 6 or 7 Fat Quarters (18 × 22 in/46 × 56 cm) of hand dyes or batiks in fresh lovely colors of your choice (I used greens, aqua, blues, red, purple, and pink tonal fabrics)

BACKGROUND: 6 yd/5.5 m of 44-in-/112-cm-wide white crisp linen or cotton fabric. If you're using wider fabric, you'll need to calculate the yardage amount based on 16 squares, each 22 in/56 cm square, for a double quilt. For a smaller quilt, use 12 squares for a single quilt, or 9 squares for a lap or toddler quilt.

BACKING: 6 yd/5.5 m of 44-in-/112-cm-wide crisp white linen, cotton, or other suitable fabric of your choice, perhaps a pretty floral print to complement the front (I used one of Amy Butler's subtle grey and white floral prints)

BATTING: 92-in-/234-cm-square piece of cotton batting; if planning to hand quilt, you might choose wool batting instead

BINDING: ¾ yd/70 cm of 44-in-/112-cm-wide crisp white linen or cotton fabric— the same fabric as your background, to give it a clean edge

DOUBLE-SIDED FUSIBLE WEBBING: Depending on width, you will need 2–3 yd/2–3 m

THREAD: White cotton thread suitable for piecing and machine quilting, plus different color cotton threads to match the colors of your appliqué

OTHER INGREDIENTS: Rotary cutter • mat • ruler • freezer paper • pencil • iron • small, sharp scissors

TEMPLATES: Motif designs for 16 flowers (in template envelope)

NOTES

- Include ¼-in/6-mm seam allowances on blocks.
- Finished block size is 21½ in/55 cm.

continued

PREPARING YOUR FABRIC

Cut sixteen 22-in-/56-cm-square pieces from the background fabric.

PREPARING YOUR MOTIFS

1. Cut the fusible webbing into sheets the same size as your Fat Quarters, 1 for each Fat Quarter.

2. Trace your motifs as closely together as possible (no need to leave any seam allowances) onto the sheets of fusible webbing. Each sheet represents a different color, so decide which pieces will be in which color and label them. Trace the large components first, choosing the main color you will feature for each flower and fill in blank spaces with any smaller components, so that you have as little wasted fabric as possible.

3. Fuse each piece of webbing, without cutting out anything, directly onto the **Wrong** side of each of your Fat Quarters. Once they've cooled, use the small, sharp scissors to carefully cut around each motif. Organize them into stacks for each flower block; this will be easier if you've labeled them.

4. Arrange the motifs for each flower on a background block. See how the colors go together; if you've forgotten any components, or don't like your color choices, replace them by tracing and cutting out more.

APPLIQUÉING

1. Place one background fabric square on your work surface, with a towel or piece of batting underneath the fabric to protect the surface from the hot iron. Press your fabric square smooth. Take the first set of motifs for one flower design and, peeling off the backings, lay them out onto your background fabric as per the layout diagram for each flower set, being sure to tuck under the pieces that are meant to be underneath. When you're happy with the configuration of your motifs, use your hot iron to gently press the motifs into place. Continue with the other squares until all the flowers have been pressed into position.

2. Take your blocks in a pile to the sewing machine. You'll be sewing around the motifs using thread matching the motifs, rather than the background fabric, so have your threads ready. For minimal thread changes, sew all of the same color before sewing the next color (i.e., do all the greens first, then yellows, etc., rather than completing one block at a time). Use a small neat zigzag or blanket stitch around each motif.

COMPLETING THE QUILT TOP

1. Once you've completed your 16 flower appliqué blocks (or less if making a smaller quilt), find a large area and lay out your blocks in a pleasing design (if using the floor, ensure that it is clean and there are no kids running through).

2. When you are happy with your layout, pin each square to the one next to it in its row and take this to the sewing machine. With cotton thread matching your background fabric, sew the pieces together and press the seams. Pin the rows together to ensure seams match up. Sew the rows together and press the entire quilt top. Your quilt top is completed.

QUILTING AND FINISHING

For instructions on making the batting and backing, see pages 34 and 36.

1. Layer the quilt top with batting and backing, and baste, using your preferred basting method (see page 37).

2. Using white thread, machine quilt with an all-over fill design (see page 40), such as the free-style leaf design I used, or your own preferred design.

3. Following the instructions on page 43, make 360 in/ 914 cm of continuous straight-cut binding; cut strips 2½ in/ 6 cm wide. Press and attach the binding in your preferred method (see page 44).

SUMMER SUNDAE

This quilt was inspired by the name of the fabric I used: Sweet. The fabric is so sugar coated and delicious that I had to make a quilt to reflect that. It's perfect for a little girl. While my preteen daughter has stated categorically that she is too old for such a sugary creation, I have noticed her glancing at it hungrily from time to time.

Finished quilt size: 67½ × 83½ in/171.5 × 212 cm

DIFFICULTY LEVEL ✱✱✱✱ This quilt has a lot of curves to piece. There are two unique blocks, and the fabric pattern pieces require you to cut them out individually with scissors. The blocks may look a little tricky with their curves, but once you get the hang of them, it isn't hard—I promise. This is a satisfying quilt to make, and making the bunting is fun, since it can be cut freehand and you can make it to your liking.

FABRIC: 10 Fat Quarters (18 × 22 in/46 × 56 cm) in assorted pretty pastel prints

BACKGROUND: 2½ yd/2.3 m of 44-in-/112-cm-wide creamy white cotton fabric

BACKING: 5 yd/4.6 m of 44-in-/112-cm-wide cotton fabric of your choice (I used a simple off-white quilting cotton)

BATTING: 75-×-90-in/191-×-229-cm of cotton batting

BINDING: ¾ yd/0.7 m of 44-in-/112-cm-wide creamy white fabric the same as your background or more of your pretty pastel fabric

THREAD: Off-white cotton thread suitable for piecing and quilting

OTHER INGREDIENTS: Freezer paper • pencil • scissors • iron

TEMPLATES: Icy-pole block and ice-cream cone block (in template envelope)

NOTES

- Use ¼-in/6-mm seam allowances throughout.
- Pieced block measures 11 × 17½ in/28 × 44.5 cm, after trimming (if needed); finished block size is 10½ × 17 in/26.5 × 43 cm.
- When piecing the top curves of both blocks, notch the curves and press the seams toward the outside edges.
- Do not cut the border strips until after you have completed the main part of the quilt top.

PREPARING YOUR FABRIC

1. Using the templates provided, trace onto freezer paper the pattern pieces for the icy-pole block and the ice-cream cone block and cut out.

2. Cut 10 ice-cream cones from print fabric (2 Fat Quarters).

3. Cut 10 icy-pole tops from print fabric (5 Fat Quarters).

4. Cut 10 ice-cream cone tops from print fabric, using left-over fabric from icy-pole tops.

5. Cut 10 icy-pole sticks from print fabric, using left-over scraps.

6. Cut 20 squares for icy-pole block (background fabric) using pattern provided.

7. Cut 10 curved tops for ice-cream cone block and 10 curved tops for the icy-pole block (background fabric).

8. Cut 10 triangles and 10 opposite triangles for ice-cream cone block (background fabric).

9. Cut 20 side strips and 10 base strips for ice-cream cone block (background fabric).

10. You will need to create your own pattern for making Popsicle buntings. Create 3 different size Popsicles by first drawing 3 rectangles, each 3 to 4 in/7 to 10 cm wide and 5 to 6 in/12 to 15 cm long, on paper. Cut out the rectangles, then round off the corners on one short side of each to make 3 different Popsicle shapes. These are your templates. Cut a minimum 50 pieces from the print fabric and 50 pieces from the background fabric. Stack in pairs (one print piece and one solid piece per pair) with **Right** sides together.

11. Stack and arrange pieces for easy organization.

MAKING THE ICE-CREAM CONE BLOCKS

1. Take your ice-cream top piece and the curved (background) top piece, find the center of each by folding in half widthwise, and finger press a crease. Pin the centers (**Right** sides together), and continue to pin the curve at 1-in/2.5-cm intervals going out to each end from the center point. Sew, notch seam, and press toward the outside edges.

2. Take your 3 triangle pieces and lay them out so you have the cone in the center with the point facing down and the 2 white pieces on either side with their points facing up and their straight edges on the outside. Pin the first 2 pieces together, sew, and press, then attach the third piece, being sure to leave ¼ in/6 mm below the cone's point for a seam allowance. Press seams.

3. Sew the top of the ice cream to the cone section and press. Then attach the side pieces and bottom piece and press the entire block.

MAKING THE ICY-POLE BLOCKS

1. Take an icy-pole top and a curved background piece, find the center of each by folding in half widthwise, and finger press a crease. Pin the centers (**Right** sides together), and continue to pin the curve at 1-in/2.5-cm intervals going out to each end from the center point. Sew, notch seam, and press toward the outside edges.

2. Sew together an icy-pole stick and 2 white square pieces. Press.

3. Sew the icy-pole to its stick by sewing the 2 sections of the block together. Press the entire block.

MAKING THE BUNTING POPSICLES

Sew around the curved sides of each bunting pair—no need to pin. You can sew them chain style. Don't sew along the straight edge. Turn them **Right** side out, through the opening along the straight edge. Finger press the seams to get a nice even curve, then press them flat with the iron.

MAKING THE QUILT TOP

1. Check block sizes and trim if necessary to 11 × 17½ in/ 28 × 44.5 cm.

2. Using the diagram as a guide, piece the blocks together in rows, pinning at intervals to match block seams, then sew the rows together. Press the entire quilt top.

3. Lay out your quilt top and measure the length. Cut 2 strips of background fabric to the length of the quilt (approximately 68½ in/174 cm) and 8 in/20 cm wide. Then measure the width of the quilt and cut 2 more strips of background fabric to the width of the quilt plus 15½ in/ 39 cm (approximately 67½ in/71 cm) and 8 in/20 cm wide. Lay these down next to the quilt top, but do not sew on just yet.

4. Lay the Popsicle shapes around your quilt border, with the curved edges facing toward the outside and the printed sides up. Once you have a pleasing arrangement and they are evenly spaced, flip them over onto the quilt top (curved edges will be facing toward the center of the quilt and solid sides will be up). Pin them onto your quilt top, with the

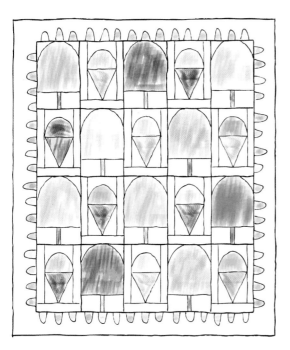

raw edges of the bunting lined up along the raw edges of the quilt top. Sew a basting stitch with a ⅛-in/3-mm seam allowance, to hold them in place.

5. Attaching the sides first, then the top and bottom, pin your border strips to the quilt top, **Right** sides together, with the bunting Popsicles sandwiched between the border and the quilt top. Sew, then press the entire quilt top and press the Popsicles so they lie over the border strips—print sides facing out.

QUILTING AND FINISHING

For instructions on making the batting and backing, see pages 34 and 36.

1. Layer the quilt top with batting and backing, and baste, using your preferred basting method (see page 37).

2. Using an off-white thread, machine quilt with an all-over fill design (see page 40; I used a squiggle design, but a stipple would work just as well). Quilt over the entire surface being careful to keep the Popsicles out of the way so you don't accidentally sew them down.

4. Follow the instructions on page 43 to make 320 in/813 cm of continuous bias binding; cut strips 2½-in/6-cm wide. Press and attach the binding in your preferred method (see page 44). Place your finished quilt on your little girl's bed and watch her snuggle under it, all warm and cozy.

SEWING CIRCLE

This is variation of a traditional Winding Ways block design, using a mixture of solid and print fabrics for a fresh summer quilt. A version of the Winding Ways block design can be attributed to Nancy Cabot (who penned a Chicago Tribune *quilt column in the '30s). However, similar designs, such as* Wheel of Mystery *and* Four Leaf Clover*, appeared in other newspapers around the same time. This version emphasizes the central circles that appear naturally as a by-product of the main design. I love the visual illusion created with all the circular designs fading in and out, giving a sense of pathways lost and found.*

Finished quilt size: 72 in/183 cm square

DIFFICULTY LEVEL ✳✳✳✳

This quilt requires precise cutting and piecing, so attention to detail is important. You'll need to do a lot of pinning and careful sewing of curves—impatience will not be rewarded, trust me. However, if you can manage all of this careful sewing, you will be rewarded with a beautiful heirloom-quality quilt.

FABRIC: 16 Fat Quarters (18 × 22 in/46 × 56 cm) of pastel print fabric (I used a selection of Amy Butler pastels)

5 Fat Quarters in solid colors (choose colors that coordinate with your pastel fabrics)

BACKGROUND: 2½ yd/2.3 m of 44-in-/112-cm-wide creamy white cotton fabric

BACKING: 4¼ yd/3.7 m of 44-in-/112-cm-wide creamy white cotton fabric

BATTING: 77-in-/196-cm-square piece of cotton batting

BINDING: ½ yd/46 cm of 44-in-/112-cm-wide fabric in a color that coordinates with your backing and background (I used pink to match the center circle)

THREAD: Neutral-color cotton thread suitable for piecing and machine quilting

OTHER INGREDIENTS: Scissors • tailor's chalk

TEMPLATES: Pattern pieces for block, leaf shape #1, quarter circle #2, in-between shape #3

NOTES

- Use ¼-in/6-mm seam allowances throughout.
- Pieced block measures 18½ in/47 cm; finished block size is 18 in/46 cm square.
- Be careful not to pull at the patches or they will stretch out of shape. If you have to unpick seams, do so carefully.
- For easier piecing, sew with the concave piece on the top and pin all around.
- When laying out the fabric pieces ready for piecing, look at the diagram to note in what position you need to sew the solid-color quarter circles.

Quilt top sewn by Chris Hayes

PREPARING YOUR FABRIC

1. Fold a print Fat Quarter into quarters, pin the leaf shape (#1) onto the top, and cut out 4 pieces at once, for a total of 64 leaf shapes from the print fabric.

2. Cut 8 quarter circles (#2) each from 4 of the solid Fat Quarters and 4 of the same shape from 1 of the last solid colors; cut 28 of the same shape from the background fabric.

3. Cut out 64 in-between shapes (#3) from the background fabric.

MAKING THE BLOCKS

1. Arrange your pieces into piles. Take a leaf-shaped piece and pin it carefully to a quarter circle, **Right** sides together (see diagram). Sew together and press the seam allowance toward the quarter circle. Do this 4 times for each block.

2. Take the leaf quarter circle units and sew an in-between piece onto one side of each unit (**Right** sides together). Press the seam allowance toward the leaf unit. Then join 2 leaf units together, being careful to match the points. Repeat for the other two leaf units.

3. Take these two halves, match up centers with the concave piece on top, and sew together (**Right** sides together). This completes your basic block.

4. Make 16 blocks total; press and trim them, if necessary, to 18½ in/47 cm square.

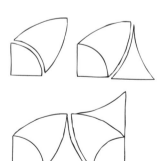
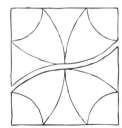

COMPLETING THE QUILT TOP

1. Lay out your blocks on a design wall if you have one or on a clean floor. Match up same-color quarter circles to make full circles; the prints can be in random order.

2. Piece the blocks together, first into pairs, then into foursomes, making sure to match up the corner points as you sew. It is important to match the corners of the colored circles perfectly to create perfect circles.

3. Press the whole quilt top flat.

QUILTING AND FINISHING

For instructions on making the batting and backing, see pages 34 and 36.

1. Layer the quilt top with batting and backing, and baste, using your preferred basting method (see page 37).

2. Using a neutral-color thread, machine quilt using an all-over free-style design (see page 40; I used a simple stipple).

3. Following the instructions on page 43, make 305 in/ 745 cm of continuous straight-cut binding; cut strips 2½ in/ 6 cm wide. Press and attach the binding in your preferred method (see page 44).

TECHNIQUES

DEGREE OF DIFFICULTY

The quilts in this book are each given a difficulty rating, as follows. As an experienced quilter you'll likely find inspiration from the quilts in this book, so start with one you like.

❋ It's a cinch: Basic piecing. If you're a beginner quilter, without much sewing experience, start with these easiest projects. You'll soon have the confidence to move up to the next level.

❋❋ Straightforward: Simple piecing and basic machine appliqué. If you already have sewing experience, but have never made a patchwork quilt before, start with these projects.

❋❋❋ Tricky: Intricate piecing and/or more demanding appliqué. If you've made a few quilts before and feel ready to tackle some trickier techniques, you may want to begin with these intermediate to demanding projects.

❋❋❋❋ Challenging: Demanding piecing techniques and/or multiple techniques. If you like a challenge and feel confident in your quilting and sewing skills, head straight for the difficult projects.

STANDARD QUILT SIZES

When you're making a quilt, you need to know how big to make it—I'm continually looking up standard quilt sizes and have found that standard sizes vary quite a bit. A baby's crib quilt can double as a wall quilt, a toddler quilt can also be a play mat or a lap quilt, and a single bed quilt could be used to throw over your double bed. If you're designing your quilt from scratch, start by measuring your bed; decide if you want the quilt to hang over the sides, or just to go to the mattress edge. In this book, finished quilt sizes are given with some idea of how you might use the quilt.

STANDARD QUILT SIZES USED IN THIS BOOK

Crib quilt: Between 36 × 36 in/91 × 91 cm and 52 × 52 in/ 132 × 132 cm.

Toddler quilt: Between 42 × 60 in/107 × 152 cm and 46 × 70 in/ 117 × 178 cm.

Single (twin) quilt: Between 64 × 86 in/163 × 218 cm and 72 × 96 in/183 × 244 cm.

Double/queen quilt: Between 70 × 88 in/178 × 224 cm and 88 × 100 in/224 × 254 cm.

Full-size mega King quilt: between 100 × 98 in/254 × 249 cm and 114 × 117 in/290 × 297 cm.

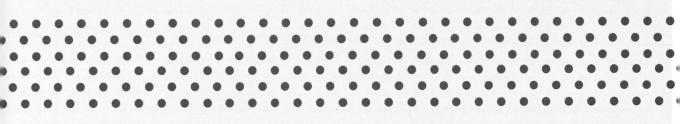

METRIC CONVERSION

As an Australian quilter, I need to be familiar with the U.S. and metric systems. I use an online metric conversion calculator (such as www.onlineconversion.com/ or www.unitednotions.com/metric_calculator.html). Hand-held metric conversion calculators are available and useful if you don't want to work online. I've provided conversions throughout the instructions in the book, but here are some standard quilting sizes in both U.S. and metric units:

- ¼ in is 6 mm (common seam allowance)
- 2½ in is 6 cm (common binding strip width, and Jelly Roll strips)
- 5 in is 12 cm (Charm Squares size)
- 10 in is 25 cm (Layer Cakes size)
- 12 in is 30.5 cm (a common basic block size)
- 1 yard of fabric is 36 in/91 cm
- 1 meter of fabric is 39.4 in/100 cm
- 44 inches is 112 cm (common quilting fabric width)

CALCULATING YARDAGE

Yardage is calculated for you in the quilt projects in this book, based upon a standard 44-in-/112-cm-wide quilting fabric (42 in/107 cm after the selvages have been removed). If you're going to alter the quilt sizes, or if you're using a different width of fabric, you'll need to recalculate how much fabric you'll need. There are some excellent online resources that help you to calculate your fabric backing, binding, and even borders (see Resources).

GLOSSARY OF TERMS

Album quilt: Appliquéd quilt with symbolic designs, often signed by the maker and made for a special occasion.

Align: To match up the raw edges or match points when sewing.

Amish quilt: A quilt made by the Amish community, who use solid fabrics with intricate hand-quilted patterns.

Appliqué: The application of a decorative design by cutting pieces of material and stitching them to a background fabric.

Appliqué glue: Also known as basting glue, a water-soluble glue that comes with a syringe applicator, which allows for the placement of controlled droplets of glue on the seam line of your fabric motif. A small glue stick also works well.

Appliqué motif: A repeated shape that is sewn onto the top of the quilt to create an overall design.

Background fabric: The foundation fabric or pieced backdrop of a quilt; the place for adding more elements of design, such as embroidery or appliqué pieces.

Backing: The layer of fabric on the back of the quilt, often utilitarian, it can be one piece of fabric or made from different pieces.

Bargello quilt technique: A style of piecing strips of fabric, which are offset from the previous strip to produce undulating designs.

Base plate, stitch plate, or throat plate: The metal plate beneath a sewing machine's needle and presser foot, with an opening for the needle to pass through as it stitches.

Basting: A way of holding the layers in a quilt together; basting can be done with pins, stitching, or basting spray.

Basting spray: A water-soluble spray glue that is used in place of pins or tacking stitches to hold the layers of the quilt together while quilting.

Batting: The stuffing, or center, of a quilt, also known as "wadding," which gives the quilt warmth and thickness.

Bearding: Synthetic batting that works its way through the fabric to the top of the quilt.

Bias: The diagonal grain across the fabric, at a 45-degree angle to the selvage.

Bias binding: Strips of fabric cut on the bias, used to bind the raw edges of the quilt.

Binding: The finished edge of a quilt, where binding, either single or double fold, is sewn over the edges of the layers of the quilt; it gives the quilt strength.

Bleeding: Loss of color in the fabric when washed; the color spreads out of its designated area and lands on the fabric near to it. Synthrapol and Retayne are brand names of products used to remove excess dyes from fabrics and to prevent them from bleeding into other fabrics.

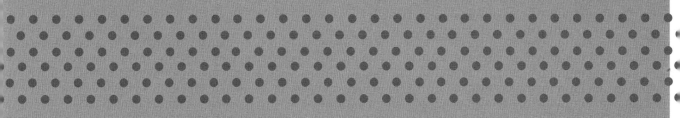

Blind stitch: Used for sewing appliqué in place by hand, or for sewing down binding; it is practically invisible.

Block: A section that is sewn together with other blocks, usually in a repeating pattern, to make the quilt top.

Blog: The shorthand term for weblog, an on-line journal where people post about their personal experiences and hobbies. There are many different thematic blogs for every topic imaginable. Craft blogs and quilting blogs are relevant here.

Blogland: A colloquial term often used to describe the virtual world of blogging.

Bobbin: In a sewing machine, the small spool located underneath the base or throat plate that holds the lower thread.

Border: Strips of plain or pieced fabric that are attached around the perimeter of your quilt and act to frame your design.

Central medallion quilt: Where a quilt has a central area that is a focus of the quilt, it is then surrounded by a patterned or plain border.

Chain piecing or chain sewing: Assembly-line piecing, where patches are aligned for sewing and fed through the machine one after another without breaking the threads between them. This allows you to sew many pieces without stopping after each one, saving both time and thread.

Charity quilts: Made by one person or a group, quilts that are either donated, auctioned, or sold to raise money for charitable causes.

Charms: Small pieces of fabric, often square but sometimes triangles or hexagons, all of the same size.

Color wheel: Hues arranged in a circular sequence—blue, blue/green, green, yellow/green, yellow, yellow/orange, orange, red/orange, red, red/purple, purple, blue/purple.

Complementary fabrics: Fabrics that have a relationship to each other, in some way—either through color, pattern, or tonal values.

Continuous binding: A length of binding strip with a minimum of joining seams.

Design wall: A wall often covered in batting or white flannel or felt, where quilters can position quilt blocks and fabric swatches, so they can view the design at a distance.

Double-fold binding: Binding that, when folded over the edge of a quilt, has a double layer of fabric.

Echo stipple quilting: Lines of quilting that outline each other and radiate out from the design, like ripples in a pond.

Embellish: Adding decorative elements to a design.

Embroidery: Fancy stitch work and decorative designs, made with needle and thread on fabric.

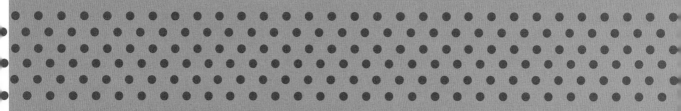

Emery pincushion: A small pincushion filled with emery, used to help keep needles and pins sharp. Emery is a very hard type of rock that when ground into a powder is used as an abrasive.

Facing: An invisible binding or lining applied to the edge of a quilt or garment for strengthening and for finishing a raw edge.

Fat Quarter: ¼-yd/46-cm cut of fabric that measures 18 × 22 in/ 46 × 56 cm instead of the typical quarter-yard cut of 9 × 44 in/ 23 × 112 cm.

Feed dogs: The metal teeth that emerge from a hole in the throat plate on a sewing machine. Their job is to grip the underside of the fabric and push it along.

Finger press: When you use your fingers to press a seam open rather than using an iron.

Foundation piecing: A method of piecing where fabric pieces are sewn to a foundation—either paper, which is then removed, or muslin, which forms part of the finished quilt. This method of piecing is used to create blocks with a complicated design or to ensure accurate results.

Free-motion quilting: Also called free-style quilting or all-over stipple quilting. It is a method of machine quilting that is done with the feed dogs on the sewing machine lowered so the quilt can then be moved in any direction; it requires an embroidery or darning foot.

Freezer paper: A heavy white paper with a plastic coating on one side; it is used in quilting or fabric stencils as a template, because it stays on fabric when ironed and is easily removed without leaving any residue.

Friendship quilt: A quilt made by friends as a gift or remembrance; each block is made by a different person and signed.

Fusible webbing: A web-like material that fuses fabric pieces together when heat activated by a warm iron.

Grain: The direction of the fabric, warp or weft. "With the grain" means parallel to the warp, or the length of the yardage.

Hand stitch or hand sew: To sew fabric with a needle and thread by hand as opposed to using a sewing machine.

Hanging sleeve: A sleeve or strip of fabric attached to the back of the quilt, enabling it to be hung on the wall while retaining its original shape.

Improvisational piecing: A type of patchwork where no pattern is used; instead it is sewn as you go, using whatever fabric you have on hand.

Jelly Roll: A sponge cake, layered with cream and jam and rolled up. In quilting terms, it refers to a pre-cut of fabric that contains 40 strips, with each strip measuring 2½ × 44 in/6 cm × 112 cm.

Layer Cake: A yummy cake with multiple layers of cake and frosting. In quilting terms, it refers to a pre-cut of fabric that contains 40 squares (10 in/25 cm).

Layout diagram: A diagram that shows how the elements of a quilt top are joined together.

Log cabin: A quilt block in which the center square is made first and rectangular "logs" are added around it, in sequence.

Meter or metre: Unit of measurement equal to 100 cm, 1.094 yards, or 39.4 inches.

Mitered corner: The corner of the binding around a quilt that is joined at a 45-degree angle.

Muslin: Plain, unbleached cotton, used as a neutral background, or as foundation fabric in quilting (also called "calico" in Australia and the United Kingdom).

Needle turn appliqué: Also called "pinch and turn" appliqué, a method used to sew the edges of the appliqué under as you sew rather than basting or ironing it in place beforehand.

Online: Refers to being connected to the Internet.

Patchwork blocks: Pieced (sewn) squares consisting of repeated shapes to create patterns.

Pearl cotton or perle cotton: An embroidery thread with a high sheen; sold in three sizes.

Piecing: Sewing pieces of fabric together to make patchwork.

Pin basting: A method of basting in which small safety pins are used to secure together all of the layers of the quilt sandwich while you quilt.

Prairie points: Squares of fabric folded into a triangle shape and used as a decorative quilt edging.

Pre-cut fabric: Pieces of fabric that are pre-cut by the manufacturer to a standard size.

Presser foot: The part of the sewing machine that sits on the fabric, pressing it as you sew. Different types of presser feet do different jobs: A darning or embroidery foot for free-motion sewing such as quilting or embroidery works effectively with the feed dogs in the down position; a walking foot walks the top of the fabric at the same time as the feed dogs walk the bottom fabric and is used for sewing multiple layers of fabric.

Prism: An optical device with a triangular shape often with an inverted opposite image.

Puckering: Folds or wrinkles in the fabric; these can occur when quilting and stitching, and are not desirable.

Quilt guild: A formal association, group, or club of people with similar interests.

Quilt sandwich: The three layers of the quilt—backing, batting, and decorative quilt top.

Quilting: Can refer to the process of making a quilt. More specifically, it is the step of stitching the quilt layers together; it adds strength and a decorative element to the quilt.

Quilting bee: A social event in which people get together to make a quilt.

Raw edge appliqué: A technique in which the edge of the appliqué motif is not turned under, but is instead sewn in place with the raw edge still showing.

Registration marks: Marks, lines, dots, or crosses placed on a pattern, ensuring accurate positioning.

Rhombus: A four-sided shape where all of the sides are equal lengths.

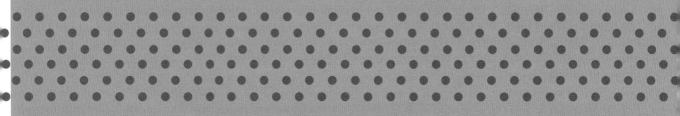

Rotary cutter: A tool with a circular blade, used to cut fabric.

Running stitch: An even hand stitch in which the stitches weave in and out of the fabric in a dashed line. Used for hand quilting.

Sashing: Strips of fabric used to separate the blocks in a quilt top. They can be plain, pieced, or appliquéd.

Seam allowance: The space between the sewn seam and the edge of the fabric; it is usually ¼ in/6 mm in quilting.

Seam ripper: A tool for removing stitches.

Selvage: Also spelled "selvedge," this is the long side edge of cloth that is reinforced to prevent unraveling. The width of fabric is measured from selvage to selvage.

Sewing notions: Sewing tools and equipment.

Single-fold binding: Binding that is made with the edges turned in toward the center; only a single fold of fabric covers the raw edge of the quilt.

Square up: To ensure that the corners are 90 degrees and the edges are completely straight.

Stipple quilting: Closely spaced, random quilting stitches done in an overall squiggly design—the quilting lines usually do not cross.

Straight-cut binding: Binding that is made with strips cut on the straight grain of the fabric.

Tacking: Also called "basting," this is a loose stitch used to temporarily hold layers of fabric together until they are stitched permanently.

Template: A cut-out pattern used to trace a design; either for piecing or appliqué patches or for tracing lines to be quilted.

Tension: A setting on the sewing machine that can be adjusted to ensure the stitches are even on the top and the bottom.

Triangle: Triangle shapes are common patchwork pieces: isosceles triangle—2 sides are equal in length; scalene triangle—all sides are unequal; right-angle triangle—one of the interior angles measures 90 degrees; equilateral triangle—all three sides are equal (also known as a regular triangle).

Unbleached cotton: Cotton fabric that has not been treated with bleaching agents or dye; it is often an off-white or beige color.

Virtual quilting bee: A group of quilters gathered in an online group to offer support, advice, and technical assistance in making a quilt.

Wreath-style quilt: A traditional quilt design made up of appliquéd motifs arranged in a circular band, often with foliage or flowers as the main feature.

Yard: A unit of measure that equals 36 in/91 cm.

RESOURCES

GUIDE TO QUILTING AND SEWING RESOURCES

For me there is really nothing better than grabbing a pile of quilting books and reading them sitting on the couch with a cup of tea. Here are some of the books I use on a regular basis for reference and inspiration.

HISTORIC QUILT REFERENCE BOOKS

The American Quilt: A History of Cloth and Comfort 1750–1950
Roderick Kiracofe and Mary Elizabeth Johnson. Clarkson Potter (2004).
If you are interested in quilting history, then this is a must-have—it has gorgeous photos and is an interesting read.

American Quilt Classics: From the collection of Patricia Cox
Patricia Cox. Maringale & Company (2001).
A beautiful book that looks at various traditional quilts and includes some patterns as well.

The Amish Quilt
Eve Wheatcroft Granick. Good Books (1989).
Full of historic Amish quilts and stories.

Going West: Quilts and Community
Smithsonian American Art Museum, Washington DC (2008).
This is a companion book to an extensive exhibition that presented fifty 19th-century quilts.

The Quilt that Walked to Golden: Women and Quilts in the Mountain West from the Overland Trail to Contemporary Colorado
Sandra Dallas. Breckling Press (2004).
A beautifully presented and researched book with beautiful historic quilts.

The Quilts of Gee's Bend: Masterpieces from a Lost Place
William Arnett, Alvia Wardlaw, Jane Livingston, and John Beardsley. Tinwood Books (2002).
Fantastic inspiration, gorgeous quilts.

Quilts 1700–2010: Hidden Histories, Untold Stories
Edited by Sue Prichard. V&A Publishing (2010).
British quilt and patchwork history.

This Old Quilt: A Heartwarming Celebration of Quilts and Quilting Memories
Margret Aldrich. Voyageur Press (2001).
Beautiful quilts and interesting stories from a variety of contributors.

Treasury of American Quilts
Cyril I. Nelson and Carter Houck. Greenwich House (1982).
More inspiring historic quilts.

QUILT PATTERN AND GENERAL SEWING REFERENCE BOOKS

The Art of Manipulating Fabric
Colette Wolff. Chilton Book Company (1996).
Invaluable source of sewing techniques.

Denyse Schmidt Quilts: 30 Colorful Quilt and Patchwork Projects
Denyse Schmidt. Chronicle Books (2005).
Simple and elegant designs for beginner quilters.

I Love Patchwork: 21 Irresistible Zakka Projects to Sew
Rashida Coleman-Hale. Interweave Press (2009).
Lots of great projects for beginner sewists.

Links to the '30s: Making the Quilts We Didn't Inherit
Kay Connors and Karen Earlywine. Martingale & Company (2009).
This is the most fantastic pattern book of traditional style quilts. The quilts are gorgeous and challenging
and the patterns and directions are very well written.

Material Obsession (books 1 and 2)
Kathy Doughty and Sarah Fielke. Stewart Tabori and Chang + Murdoch Books (2008/2009).
Two incredible quilt books, by two incredible Australian quilters.

The Modern Quilt Workshop: Patterns, Techniques, and Designs from the Funquilts Studio
Bill Kerr and Weeks Ringle. Quarry Books (2005).
A wealth of quilting information, great tips, and modern designs.

Quilter's Complete Guide
Marianne Fons and Liz Porter. Oxmoor House (2001).
A must-have book for beginner quilters.

Quilting for Peace: Make the World a Better Place One Stitch at a Time
Katherine Bell. STC Craft/A Melanie Falick Book (2009).
Stories and patterns of quilting for charity.

The Sewing Bible: A Modern Manual of Practical and Decorative Sewing Techniques
Ruth Singer. Potter Craft (2008).
Fantastic detailed overview of many basic and more complex sewing techniques.

200 Quilting Tips, Techniques & Trade Secrets
Susan Briscoe. Sally Milner Publishing (2009).
So many quilting tips and tricks all in one place.

Whip Up Mini Quilts
Kathreen Ricketson. Chronicle Books (2010).
My quilting book—for mini quilt enthusiasts and beginner quilters.

SEWING, QUILTING, AND CRAFTY BLOGS WITH TIPS AND TUTORIALS AND JUST FABULOUS INSPIRATION AND IDEAS

www.angrychicken.typepad.com

www.aquiltisnice.blogspot.com

www.artgalleryfabrics.typepad.com

blog.modernacorn.com

www.crazymomquilts.blogspot.com

www.dontlooknow.typepad.com

www.filminthefridge.com

www.handmadebyalissa.com

www.heatherbailey.typepad.com

www.jaybirdquilts.com

www.meetmeatmikes.blogspot.com

www.modabakeshop.com

www.mollychicken.blogs.com

www.mrsschmenkmanquilts.wordpress.com

www.ohfransson.com

www.patchandi.blogspot.com

www.pinkchalkstudio.com/blog/

www.psiquilt.com

www.redpepperquilts.com

www.sewmamasew.com/blog2/

www.sometimescrafter.blogspot.com

www.spiritcloth.typepad.com

www.stitchindye.blogspot.com

www.tallgrassprairiestudio.blogspot.com

www.threekitchenfairies.typepad.com

www.treefalldesign.typepad.com

MORE

www.hickoryhillquilts.com/fabric-calculator.htm
Calculating yardage and binding.

www.onlineconversion.com/ or
www.unitednotions.com/metric_calculator.html
Online metric conversion calculator.

www.quiltersbuzz.com
The latest in quilting and fabric news.

www.themodernquiltguild.com
Home of the modern quilt guild.

www.trueup.net
Fabric addiction.

whipup.net
Handcraft in a hectic world.

www.whipup.net/2006/03/01/stickin-it-to-the-pincushion/
Whipup pincushion tutorial.

JOIN

Join a virtual quilting bee

Check in at the Quilting Bee Blocks Flickr group, where you can add pictures of quilt blocks made for virtual quilting bees and check the discussion board for a list of virtual quilting bees, with new groups being added all the time: www.flickr.com/groups/quiltingbeeblocks/discuss/

Join a swap

Organize your swaps online: www.swap-bot.com

FABRIC AND THREAD RESOURCES

Coats & Clark
www.coatsandclark.com

Free Spirit Fabric
www.freespiritfabric.com

Ink & Spindle (independent designers)
www.inkandspindle.com

Island Batik
www.islandbatik.com

Lecien fabric
www.lecien.co.jp/en/hobby/index.html

Michael Miller Fabrics
www.michaelmillerfabrics.com

Moda Fabrics from United Notions
www.unitednotions.com

Robert Kaufman Fabrics
www.robertkaufman.com

Westminster Fabrics (and now thread, too)
www.westminsterfabrics.com

Windham Fabrics
www.windhamfabrics.com

YLI Corp. (beautiful hand-quilting threads)
www.ylicorp.com

FABRIC DESIGNERS' BLOGS/WEBSITES

Amy Butler
www.amybutlerdesign.com

Anna Maria Horner
www.annamariahorner.com

French General
www. frenchgeneral.blogspot.com

Lauren + Jessi Jung
www. laurenandjessiblog.com

Minick and Simpson
www. minickandsimpson.blogspot.com

Paula Prass
www. paulaprass.blogspot.com

Tula Pink
www.tulapink.com

INDEX

QUILT BLOCKS

5 FLAVORS
foundation block

(50% scale)

RHOMBUS
foundation block

(50% scale)

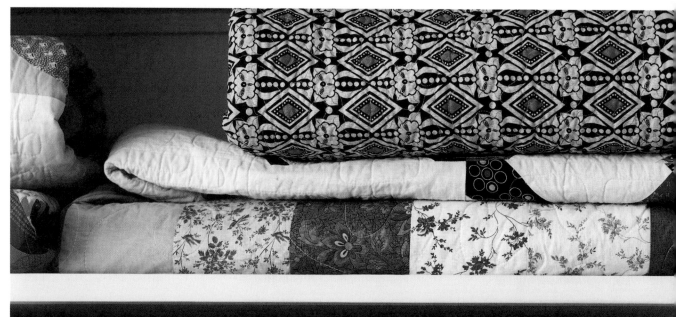

ACKNOWLEDGMENTS

I would like to dedicate this book to my female ancestors, including my great-grandmother Eliza, whose life was short but whose legacy was long; even though her 6 children were orphaned at a young age, she had passed on to them her skills as a fine seamstress. At the tender age of 10, my grandmother Gertrude had already learned the fine art of lace crochet, and continued to knit, crochet, sew, and bake for her family her whole life. It was through her that I learned a multitude of sewing tricks and tips and discovered my lifelong love of fabric collecting. And my mother, Janette, whose everyday creativity and frugality while raising me and my brothers taught me to value the little things. I grew up among making-do and making stuff as an everyday part of life thanks to her.

I have many people to thank for this book—my friends and family who supported me along the way and put up with my not returning calls and ignoring them for the better part of a year, and who listened attentively as I went on and on about quilting. Thank you to my colleagues who let me take time off to concentrate on the book as I was nearing my deadline. A belated thank-you to my art school mentors, Denise Ferris and Martyn Jolly, who told me that they knew that art would always be a part of my life—that thought has stuck with me through the creatively dry years of early motherhood and nurtured me as I began to create again. Thank you to the team at Chronicle Books: my editor, Laura Lee Mattingly, all the wonderful technical editors and designers who made sense of my instructions and designs while at the same time giving me freedom to express myself. Also thank you to photographer John Paul Urizar and his beautiful son Pablo, stylist Stephanie Powell, and their team for helping make the quilts look so beautiful. And a big cheery virtual hug to my agent, Courtney Miller-Callihan, whose gentle guidance gives me the confidence to put pen to my ideas.

I want to especially thank my mother-in-law, Dace Shugg, who gave an enormous amount of support and help with this book, calculating all the metric conversions and reading through the early manuscript, and who facilitated the sewing of many of the 65 Roses blocks. I would like to thank the many others who made blocks for the 65 Roses Charity Quilt: Sue Aliern, Annette Harrigan, Anne (Craft Gossip), Muriel Bowler, Wendy Buddle and the McLean Patchwork & Quilting group, Sandi Butler (Embroideroo), Camille Condon, Chowne (couchy 09), Tina Crowe, Katia D, Doreen, Tracy & Ginny, Joan Farlow, Fay Farnham, Fran (Lovely little sweet peas), Marjory Francombe, Victoria Gertenbach, Claudette Hough, Beverly Hunn, Janine Johnson, Lori Kay, Beth Keen, Salihand Langesen, Leanne, Sarah McGinnes, Helen McNamara, Andrea Medwin, Diana Murdoch, Sarah O'Halloran, Elaine Parker, Dianne Rogers, Vikki Sandford, Alison Sheehan, V. Shimmin, Patricia Spiers, Sonia Stanton, Zoe Stranger, Caroline (Stompergirl), A. Teniswood-Harvey, Penny Vanderwal, Liga Veska, Jacqueline Warrick, and Willy wag tail.